THE TEA
Winning Tools and Tactics for Successful Workouts

THE TEAM TRAINER
Winning Tools and Tactics for Successful Workouts

William I. Gorden

Erica L. Nagel

Scott A. Myers

Carole A. Barbato

AMERICAN SOCIETY FOR TRAINING AND DEVELOPMENT

1640 KING STREET
BOX 1443
ALEXANDRIA, VIRGINIA
22313-2043

Professional Publishing®
Chicago • London • Singapore

©Richard D. Irwin, a Times Mirror Higher Education Group, Inc. company, 1996

All rights reserved. No part of this publication may be reproduced, stored in a retrieval system, or transmitted, in any form or by any means, electronic, mechanical, photocopying, recording, or otherwise, without the prior written permission of the publisher.

Irwin Book Team

Senior sponsoring editor: *Cynthia A. Zigmund*
Marketing manager: *Kelly Sheridan*
Production supervisor: *Dina L. Treadaway*
Assistant manager, desktop services: *Jon Christopher*
Project editor: *Ethel Shiell*
Jacket designer: *Hunter Design*
Art studio: *Electronic Publishing Services, Inc.*
Compositor: *Electronic Publishing Services, Inc.*
Typeface: *10/12 Palatino*
Printer: *Malloy Lithographing, Inc.*

Times Mirror
Higher Education Group

Library of Congress Cataloging-in-Publication Data

The Team trainer : winning tools and tactics for successful workouts
 / William I. Gorden . . . [et.al.].
      p.   cm.
     Copublished with American Society for Training and Development.
     Includes bibliographical references and index.
     ISBN 0-7863-0511-8
    1. Work groups—Handbooks, manuals, etc. 2. Employees—Training
of—Handbooks, manuals, etc.   I. Gorden, William I., 1929–
HD66.T427 1996
658.3´124—dc20   95-4708

Printed in the United States of America
1 2 3 4 5 6 7 8 9 0 ML 2 1 0 9 8 7 6 5

About the Authors

William I. Gorden earned his M.S. and Ph.D. degrees from Purdue University. He did postdoctoral work at Northwestern, Florida State, and Utah universities. He has been on the faculties of Purdue University, Berry College, Southwest Texas University, and Kent State University, and a visiting professor at Luven University, Belgium. He has lectured at Lund University, Sweden, and has completed a study of the Swedish work environment. His travels in the Middle East and Pacific Rim have enlarged his understanding of work in widely diverse cultures. Bill's special areas of interest and research include quality improvement, ethics, employee voice, superior–subordinate interaction, organizational rhetoric, and work-group communication. He has interviewed managers and employees involved with quality improvement in major corporations, government agencies, and nonprofit organizations from coast to coast. Recently, he produced a videotape report of a year-long team training he and a colleague did for a General Electric plant. He has conducted seminars from Augusta, Georgia, to Hilo, Hawaii.

Erica L. Nagel is completing her master's degree in organizational communication at Kent State University. Her current research interests are focused on her thesis, directed by William I. Gorden, which explores organizational change and resistance to change. Through the use of individual interviews and focus groups, she examined the implementation of a smoke-free policy on a university campus as an organizationwide change and the compliance gaining and resistance strategies used during the implementation. Her other research interests include organizational training and development. She is currently employed at the Council for Adult and Experiential Learning in Cleveland, Ohio, whose primary objective is to link adults in the work force with education and training opportunities. She owes immeasurable thanks to her parents, Ronni and Stu, and her brother, Greg, for their constant love and support. She also wants to pay tribute to her Grandfather Lou. He brought a special meaning to the word "team" through his involvement in sports and his wonderful team spirit in her family.

Scott A. Myers (Ph.D., Kent State University, 1995) has many research interests, which include socialization, mentor–protege relationships, and communication climate. His research has appeared in *Western Journal of Communication*, *Communication Research Reports*, *The Speech Communication Teacher*, and *Journal of Graduate Teaching Assistant Development*. His future plans include becoming an administrator at the university level.

Carole A. Barbato (Ph.D., Kent State University, 1994) is an assistant professor of communication studies at Kent State University, East Liverpool Campus. Carole has had a long-time interest in the study of small group behavior ever since she took her first undergraduate small groups course taught by William I. Gorden. Dr. Gorden's enthusiasm and intense curiosity about small group behavior inspired her then and continues to be an inspiration today. She has committed her research effort to understanding small group behavior. This interest led to her dissertation study, which explored the role of argumentative behavior and beliefs on the process and product of small decision-making groups. She has published articles in *Human Communication*

Research, *Communication Quarterly*, *Communication Research*, and *The Gerontologist*. When she is not teaching, conducting research, or writing, she enjoys indoor and outdoor gardening. She resides in Poland, Ohio, with her husband Patrick and their perfect daughter, Alissa. Alissa and Pat keep life in perspective for Carole, reminding her of what is really important in life—the most important group of all—family.

Preface

Let us be clear that by the word *trainer* we do not mean an instructor who whips trainees into shape. Trainers, at their best, facilitate collaborative learning. They educate. They enable seminar participants and course members to better understand theory and to develop skills by doing. Today's trainers are not lion trainers. To try such tactics simply will not work because today's workers, managers, and publics are not pussycats.

A successful workout associated with the workplace, like a workout in gym, is one in which your body is strengthened, your mind is enlivened, and your spirit is refreshed. A workout is not something someone can do for you. Only you can warm up and stretch your muscles, only you can get your heart pumping and cardiovascular system exercised. You alone? No.

To be sure a workout is something only you can do, yet workouts are rarely solo activities. Walk into any sports center and you will see that people feel the need to exercise together. And that is particularly true when it comes to team sports and work organizations.

The workout has been adopted into the training language and practice of work organizations. General Electric and other large corporations use workouts to bring together work groups, staff, and managers in numbers from 20 to 100 people. For three to five days, those present in workout sessions confront and concentrate on current production and service problems.

The key focus in these sessions is discovery of how they and their co-workers are troublesome or helpful to their own and other work groups. Workout participants discover how difficult it is to do high-quality work when some fail to listen, and how helpful it is when they follow up on problems.

The workout is purposeful. It is interactive and dynamic. It is a time of self-discovery, interpersonal skill development, and team building. It is a time of learning and practice with tools and tactics needed for cooperative endeavor. This will become increasingly understood as you read on and as you take part in the many Workouts in Part II of this book.

The Evolution of the Book

The first draft of *The Team Trainer* grew out of a graduate communication studies seminar about teamwork and training. The activities were trial tested within the seminar and then in training sessions within the workplace.

The communication studies teamwork and training seminar participants wrote the first draft, which was one of many such seminars Bill Gorden designed to train those employed in various organizations. Seminar topics included how to create academic games, time management, interpersonal communication, nonverbal communication, communication ethics, collaborative learning, presentational speaking, quality improvement, and most of all, teamwork. They were conducted across the United States, from Georgia to Hawaii, and as far away as Bahrain, Sweden, and Belgium. The seminars varied in length, from one day to a year and a half.

The team of Bill Gorden, Erica Nagel, Scott Myers, and Carole Barbato, which co-authored *The Team Trainer*, did not do all of its work in committee. The planning, assignments, and working agreement were the result of numerous meetings that spanned over a year. The writing and editing was completed individually and each reviewed the others' work.

Erica Nagel's organization and creativity focused on the coordination, formatting, and editing of the text. Scott Myers' preciseness and genius focused on the editing of the text and preparation of the training exercises. Erica and Scott also were participants in the original seminar and authors of some of the exercises from which this text was born. Carole Barbato's keen knowledge of small group literature brought to life studies of teamwork in the work environment. She too took on the editing and preparation of the text and added insights and debriefing questions to the workouts. Gorden's initial vision and consistent guidance through this team effort, along with his opening chapters, have been a crucial part of bringing *The Team Trainer* to its finished form. We think and speak of ourselves as a team. Various tasks were assigned to those whose talents were best suited to them. Leadership was shared. In short, we practiced what we preach.

The people who initially designed several of the experiential training activities during the teamwork training seminar and should be acknowledged are Anne Zaphiris, Rebecca Merkin, Mike Russell, Vicky Saari, and Selma Ford.

We especially appreciate the excellent work done by the Irwin Professional Publishing team: Senior Editor, Cynthia Zigmund; Project Editor, Ethel Shiell; Marketing Manager, Kelly Sheriden; and Production Supervisor, Dina Treadaway.

How to Use this Book

Here are a few suggestions for using *The Team Trainer*. We believe that this text can be used in various settings. These include:

- Organizations that are training their members to work better in teams. These include both companies that manufacture goods and deliver services and not-for-profit associations such as churches, synagogues, environmental agencies, civic groups, unions, and those with educational and political purposes.
- College courses designed to develop understanding and skills in group processes. These courses may be housed within communication, sociology, psychology, and business departments.
- Technical schools and community colleges engaged in developing career-oriented skills.

The Team Trainer is meant to be used either as the main resource or as a complementary text for a class or seminar in team building, or in courses pertaining to group communication and professional communication. It may be used in part or whole, depending on the needs of a particular situation.

Part I *Foundations for Teamwork* can be read and discussed chapter by chapter. Trainers and instructors may find it useful to assign panels to present discussion of each of the six chapters.

Part II *Experiential Workouts for Team Building* can be used in conjunction with the chapters in Part I, or various activities may be selected as the trainer/instructor sees fit. By having 23 workouts from which to choose, a trainer will be able to provide seminar participants with appropriate group communication knowledge and skills.

Part III *Roots of Work Group Research* is especially helpful to trainers and instructors who want to acquaint participants with the rich history of group research. Very few texts so vividly describe group dynamics research and team building efforts that have been important in the workplace. These chapters, like those in Part I, may be assigned to panels for discussion, or may be studied individually.

The Team Trainer is meant to be *used*. By this, we mean that participants are expected to take notes and write in it. In addition, the seminar leader may wish to collect the text and review the responses to the workouts. Those who first use this text can also use the experiential workouts to develop teamwork skills in their own workplace and not-for-profit organizations.

Write or call to tell us how you are using *The Team Trainer*.

Bill Gorden
Erica Nagel
Scott Myers
Carole Barbato

Contents

Part I
FOUNDATIONS FOR TEAMWORK   1

Chapter One
GIVE ME A T...   3

Chapter Two
HIGHLY EFFECTIVE TEAMS   11

Chapter Three
FROM QUALITY CIRCLES TO SELF-DIRECTED WORK GROUPS   15

Chapter Four
THE BENCHMARK PROCESS   19

Chapter Five
UNDERSTANDING TEAM DYNAMICS   21

Chapter Six
BEFORE TEAM TRAINING— THE GO/NO GO DECISION   27

Part II
EXPERIENTIAL WORKOUTS FOR TEAM BUILDING   33

Chapter Seven
NOTE TO THE TRAINER-FACILITATOR: HOW TO USE PART II   35

THE BIG PICTURE   39

Chapter Eight
HOW IS OUR WORKPLACE A SYSTEM?   41
Workout: What Is a System? 43

Chapter Nine
HOW DOES OUR SYSTEM OPERATE?   45
Workout: Work at Work, 47

Chapter Ten
WE'RE ALL IN THIS TOGETHER　49
Workout: Piecing It Together, 50

Chapter Eleven
AND NOW FOR THE WEATHER…　51
Workout: Rain, Rain, Go Away! 53

Chapter Twelve
UNCOMMON SENSE　55
Workout: Dominos and Interdependence, 56
Workout: Get All You Can, 57

MOTIVATION　59

Chapter Thirteen
TEAMWORK　61
Workout: Brainstorming, 63

Chapter Fourteen
HEAD OVER HEELS　65
Workout: Go(al) Ahead! 66

Chapter Fifteen
IT BEGINS WITH ME　67
Workout: Just for Today, 69

Chapter Sixteen
PRESENTATIONS MADE EASY　71
Workout: Ready, Set, Go! 72

LISTENING　75

Chapter Seventeen
LISTENING IS A TEAM EFFORT　77
Workout: Listen and You Will Hear, 79

Chapter Eighteen
WHEN THE BALL IS IN YOUR COURT　81
Workout: Bouncing Messages, 83

Chapter Nineteen
IMPROVING YOUR TEAM'S LISTENING SKILLS　85
Workout: It Takes Three, 87

ROLES — 89

Chapter Twenty
FRIENDLY TEAMWORK — 91
Workout: Innerview, 93

Chapter Twenty-One
CLASH, BANG, BOOM! — 95
Workout: Roll with Roles, 96

Chapter Twenty-Two
THE TEAM THAT PLAYS TOGETHER STAYS TOGETHER — 99
Workout: The Role of Roles, 100

DECISION MAKING — 103

Chapter Twenty-Three
CAN THIS DECISION BE MADE? — 105
Workout: The Good, the Bad, the Others, 106

Chapter Twenty-Four
A TOOL KIT FOR PROBLEM SOLVING — 109
Workout: Just Do It, 111

Chapter Twenty-Five
WHEN PEOPLE AGREE — 113
Workout: Decision by Design, 114

Chapter Twenty-Six
TEAMTHINK — 115
Workout: Think, Team! 117

GOAL SETTING — 119

Chapter Twenty-Seven
TRANSFORMING WORK INTO A VISION OF LOVE — 121
Workout: Vision of LOVE: Learning, Observing, and Validating Our Existence, 123

THE NONVERBAL ELEMENT — 125

Chapter Twenty-Eight
SPACE: THE FINAL FRONTIER — 127
Workout: Do Not Cross, 129

Chapter Twenty-Nine
THE SMILE DOESN'T MEAN I'M HAPPY   131
Workout: A Smile or a Frown? 132

Part III
ROOTS OF WORK GROUP RESEARCH   133

Chapter Thirty
PIONEERING WORK GROUP RESEARCH: THE 1920s AND 1930s   135
Our Legacy of Groups in the Workplace, 135
Philadelphia Textile Mill, 136
Hawthorne Experiments, 137
The ABC Shoe Factory, 139

Chapter Thirty-One
WORK GROUP ACTION RESEARCH IN THE 1940s   143
The Chicago Factory Studies, 143
The Aircraft Studies, 145
The Harwood Pajama Factory Study, 145

Chapter Thirty-Two
STUDIES OF WORK GROUPS IN THE 1950s   149
Assembly-Line Study, 149
The Cash Posters Study, 150
Midwest Machine Company: Group Cohesiveness Study, 151

Chapter Thirty-Three
STUDIES OF WORK GROUPS IN THE 1960s   153
Harwood Revisited, 153
Norwegian Shoe Factory, 154
Summary of the Group Participation Studies, 155
Tavistock Institute, 155
National Training Laboratories: T-groups, 157

Chapter Thirty-Four
WORK GROUP ACTION RESEARCH IN MORE RECENT TIMES   161
Quality Circles and Total Quality Management Movement, 161
Socio-technical Experiments of the Scandinavian Countries, 164
The United States Saturn Experience, 166
Employee Ownership Programs, 167
Epilogue, 167

Appendixes *171*

    Appendix A "WORK AT WORK" AND "ROLL WITH ROLES" NOTECARDS   *173*

    Appendix B "WORK AT WORK" AND "ROLL WITH ROLES" SHEET   *175*

    Appendix C "PIECING IT TOGETHER" GAMEBOARD AND PUZZLE PIECES   *177*

    Appendix D "LISTEN AND YOU WILL HEAR" SCRIPT   *179*

    Appendix E "THE ROLE OF ROLES" NOTECARDS   *181*

    Appendix F "DO NOT CROSS" NOTECARDS   *183*

    Appendix G "A SMILE OR A FROWN?" NOTECARDS   *185*

Resources *187*

Index *193*

THE TEAM TRAINER
Winning Tools and Tactics
for Successful Workouts

PART I FOUNDATIONS FOR TEAMWORK

Chapter One

Give Me a T...

TEAM ... TEAM ... TEAM ... TEAM!!! **T**ogether **E**veryone **A**ccomplishes **M**ore. We learn to play together in teams, to compete, and to cooperate to better compete. Teams teach us that we can accomplish more by working together. We learn that none of us is as smart as all of us.

What We Have Learned from Playing Together

Team is a powerful word. Its ancient roots are in agriculture as in two or more beasts of burden harnessed together for work; its more recent roots are in play, in team sports. The team concept helps structure the way we think about ourselves in relation to others. The influence of team sports on our culture cannot easily be overestimated. Team sports encourage traits of loyalty, discipline, concern for doing something well, cooperation, and a never-say-die attitude.

Team sports teach us that we must take turns, that we must be willing to play assigned positions, and that we must become skilled at our assigned positions. Team coaches expect an eagerness to follow orders. Members of a team develop taken-for-granted expectations of each other.

Teams often represent a larger organization. Team members expect backing. Cheerleaders, team songs, mascots, fans, emblems, and flags evoke devotion and organizational identification. There is a wonderful sense of belonging felt in teamness and special pride in being on and in backing a winning team. In teams, we experience human bonding beyond the family. In teams, we rise above self-interest to appreciate mutual concern and vicariousness. In teams, we learn the frustrations and the joys of cooperative endeavor.

Of what sports teams are you or were you part?

Not Blind to Team's Evils

But let us not be blind to the unfavorable connotations that have soiled the *team* word. Team sports imply opposition and competition. Competition motivates us to strive to do whatever we do better, but competition also brings out our evil selves. Even a little familiarity with team sports provides ample evidence of the devil side of teamness: some players physically bash other players, such as in hockey and football, resulting in life-long injuries; some players play dirty; some coaches spy on other teams and steal their playbooks; many fans and coaches rabidly harass and denounce referees and applaud opponents' errors; and most of us support our team when it is winning and berate it when it is losing. A school's, city's, state's, and country's ego and sense of self-worth can be wrapped up in winning and losing.

Winning becomes so important to parents and coaches, even in Little League, that the fun of play can be lost for the kids. The drive to win leads to playing only the best players and keeping those with less talent on the bench. Coaches tend to microcoach, assuming they should call all plays. Players are supposed to do what they are told. The win-at-all-costs attitude too often causes players to play with injuries and to use drugs to enhance physical strength.

There are drawbacks to team structures. Doing business by committee can be as inefficient and as frustrating as is democracy in the larger society. An organization sometimes becomes so enamored with teamness that little else is done than talk. Teams also open the floodgates of interpersonal conflict, finger pointing, and defused responsibility. All this could be avoided, some will argue, if team stuff is forgotten, if someone takes charge and gives orders.

Teams involve frequent communication, and communication can be stressful. Team building, therefore, requires development of interpersonal skills as well as training in group problem solving.

The Downside to Teamthink

There is also the downside of teamthink. Teamthink fosters a "we are right and good—they are wrong and bad" mindedness. After-the-game rationalization blames others for one's mistakes and lack of ability. Someone has to take the blame, so good coaches are replaced after a string of losses. Team competition leads to viewing opponents as enemies. Teamthink puts down players who dare to differ about how the game should be played. Teamthink is so concerned about pulling together that it discounts self-criticism.

Perhaps the most serious downside of teamness is its unquestioning acceptance of who gives the orders. Even in high school and college, many coaches rule like dictators. Owners of professional sport teams buy and sell players and coaches at outrageous salaries. There is something very undemocratic about that.

Team Abuse in the Workplace

The T-word has also been misused within the workplace. Management too often has invoked teamness to improve efficiency and productivity without genuinely sharing power and profits. Employees who question policies or practices are told that they must be flexible; to question the organization is not good team spirit. Team play may be used to mean putting in long hours and making extraordinary sacrifice. Some companies who pay by the hour pressure their employees, in the name of team spirit, to work off the clock so they do not have to pay overtime.

At other times, the *team* word is used to tell employees that they should be satisfied to stay in a particular position and that only prima donnas want special treatment—to get ahead and to not be cut, one must go along with the flow and not make waves. They are told that team players must not complain. Employees who argue are troublemakers. Those who comply are happy campers.

Team players must make their production and sales quotas. They must fit into the system and work hard for merit, but realize that not everyone can come out on top. Ironically, at the same time management is invoking a team-way of doing things, appraisal of individual performance rather than team performance is usually the basis for promotions, salary, and bonuses. Team players are supposed to accept cuts in wages and plant shut-downs even when executives are taking more and more compensation. Managers rarely see union members as part of the management team. The win-win reward that comes from working together for the good of all is more fiction than fact.

Wise Use of Teams

Despite these negative connotations to the T-word, a wise use of teams is gaining ground. Global competition has forced corporate America to reexamine how it manages. This reexamination has led to the unanimous conclusion that bosses do not know what is best—that if America is to compete, we must practice what we learned on the playground and on the ballfield, that teamwork is superior to bossing.

Teamwork is not something that can be ordered, begged, borrowed, or bought. Teamwork in a workplace only comes about when management and employees together feel the need for it and can see its advantages.

Current emphasis on team building in corporate America seeks to lessen the power of the boss and to empower the work unit. Bosses are taught not to micromanage. Work teams are trained to think and to become self-managed. Layers of management are being cut, and the organizational hierarchy is being flattened. Profit sharing and stock options are seen as good for more than just those at the top.

A lot of attention is now focused on the beneficial effects of team building in organizations. The difference between a work unit and a team is that a work unit does not deliberate together. Individual co-workers on an auto assembly line may each do certain tasks that culminate in a car being driven off the line every 30 minutes. Sixty musicians may each play as a director produces a symphony.

How are teams used in your workplace?

Work Groups Are Different from Teams

Individuals in work groups do what they are told to do. Work groups are run by leaders who keep talk to a minimum, make assignments, and monitor performance. Although individual performance of a work unit can be cumulative in results, teamness is not a definition that is appropriate.

Work teams are different from work groups in many ways. Whereas work groups focus on individual accountability, work teams focus on mutual accountability and collective performance. Whereas members of work groups may compete for individual performance approval, team members deliberate on how teams can contribute to the organization. Whereas work groups speak as individuals, team conversations are open ended and problem solving is ongoing.

Size of Teams

The size of work units varies from few people to many people. In organizational jargon, the span of control of a superior of a work group may be as few as 3 and possibly as large as 100. Groups that make policies are sometimes quite large. State and national legislative bodies may number in the hundreds. Teams, because of their interaction in shaping and implementing their goals, are much smaller than large work groups.

Teams may be as few as two members. A two-member team might be a boss and secretary. Most work teams have no more than 10 members. Some are slightly larger. A 14-member team might be the number of individuals required to assemble a machine. Exact numbers are arbitrary, but it is difficult to listen to every team member when the size of the team gets too large.

Team Goals

Ongoing conversations center on what is the charge given to the team. A team's charge or assignment comes from one of three sources: (l) an executive committee, board, or manager; (2) a large body, such as a professional association's legislative body; or (3) the team itself.

The first responsibility of a newly formed team is to determine if the team has the people on it needed to accomplish the assignment. Therefore, the opening discussion of a group revolves around its assignment. A natural anxiety springs from assignments that are vague, which they often are. Tension is especially keen when a team doubts that an assignment is attainable. Team members inevitably mumble, fumble, and sometimes grumble while trying to determine: What are we supposed to do? And is it possible?

Effective teams set both long- and short-term goals, and deliberate how these goals can best be realized. Teams share leadership and followership roles. Teams frequently monitor their progress and discuss how well they are working as a team. Work teams are best defined by their behavior. Those on teams speak of themselves as a team. They set goals and make plans to accomplish them. They possess or seek to acquire the skills necessary to carry out purposeful activities. They hold themselves accountable.

The life of teams depends on the kind of teams they are and the charge they have been given or that they have taken. Ad hoc teams are those generally charged with short time frames. At the other extreme, natural work groups may evolve into teams that continue across the years, even when some retire and new members join. An examination of how this occurs in the workplace is discussed in Part III.

Kinds of Teams

Jon Katzenbach and Douglas Smith, co-authors of *The Wisdom of Teams*, describe three kinds of teams: teams that recommend things, teams that run things, and teams that make things.

Teams that recommend include task forces, project groups, executive steering committees, boards of directors, and union executive committees. Teams that recommend and make policy decisions are more effective if they are representative of those who must consider and carry out their recommendations and policies.

Teams that run things are rare because supervisors of work units fail to think of themselves as team members. But teams that run things are necessary if organizational barriers to continuous quality improvement are to be broken down.

Teams that make or do things include functional groups such as manufacturing, marketing, sales, and service.

Characteristic Behavior of Teams at Work

A firm that has a team environment is characterized by many of the following behaviors: Top management asks for subordinates' input. Subordinates have confidence in the leadership. Motivation is high. Attitudes toward the organization and its goals are positive. Communication is open and extensive. Information flows freely throughout the levels of the organization. Decision making and control generally occur at all levels through group processes. The emphasis is on self-control and problem solving. Goal setting and performance standards are high but realistic. Moreover, there is a commitment for career development through training and job enlargement. Participation is the key to everything.

If teams are to be optimally effective, they must *be* the structure in use of a workplace. Every workplace has an organizational chart with a chain of authority. A team structure in use differs from a charted chain of command. Clusters of interdependent co-workers can and should be organized into overlapping teams. Those teams may be organized around products.

At a General Electric lamp plant, each product group, such as its sodium Lucalox lamp group, has a management team that meets frequently. Beneath each product management team in this nonunion plant are several natural work-group teams of hourly employees. In addition, there are voluntary quality circles that work on specific projects related to their regular assignments. One quality circle that named itself the Trouble Shooters examined several boxes of defective bulbs. They diagnosed the causes of these defects. At another meeting, they decided to train workers in order to prevent those defects caused by worker error. They also talked with the mechanics to find ways to correct defects caused by machines.

The work of these teams revolves around production matters: lamp defects, waste, quality control, and customer dissatisfaction. Shop teams are bolstered by frequent contact with members of the management team. Managers, individually and sometimes with a manager of other products, walk along production lines on every shift, three times a day, to monitor and confer with those on the shop floor. Also, each day there are 11-minute stand-up meetings of work units to discuss the day's work.

Paradoxically, because team structures force managers to give up some of their control, less supervision is necessary. Teams are potentially more efficient and productive because teamness develops self-sufficiency. Self-managed teams encourage workers to think for themselves, anticipate problems, and implement improvements, thereby improving the quality of both the product and employees' work life. Self-managed teams may arrange schedules, set profit targets, and have a voice in purchasing materials and equipment. Where teams are given power, supervision is less.

What behaviors are characteristic of your work group?

Some Rough Times in Work Teams

XEL Communications Inc.'s rocky venture into teamness illustrates how difficult the transition to democratic thinking can be. The Association for Manufacturing chose to feature XEL, the 180-employee company in Aurora, Colorado, in a video on team-based management. XEL, however, was not chosen because everything runs smoothly.

In traditionally managed companies, the boss steps in to separate warring parties or in some cases to discipline them. Under team management, spats and grudges must be handled by the team; if disputes do not get settled, production suffers. In one instance, however, XEL Vice President John Puckett did intervene after he got wind of an argument between the stockroom's team attendance taker and an employee who reported in 20 minutes late. He also had complaints about not being well served from the stockroom's internal customers.

Upon further investigation, he found that employees in the stockroom had covered for each other's cheating on time cards. The result was that team-based management in the stockroom came to an abrupt halt. The abusers were fired, and a stockroom supervisor with full disciplinary authority was appointed.

In another instance, a XEL team, known as the Red Team, suffered from conflict not unlike the stockroom. Puckett assigned a facilitator to oversee the team. This annoyed the Red Team. But the Red Team "got its act together" and soon had no need for a facilitator, and Puckett withdrew him. These examples drawn from XEL Communications illustrate that backtracking to autocratic management sometimes occurs in the transition to team-based management.

Most workers feel team structures are worth the effort, even when limited shifts are made toward democracy in the workplace. In teams, they have a better opportunity to make a difference. No longer are they silent, anonymous workers. Rather, they have an influence on the fate of the company.

Some Good Times for Work Teams

Vans, a shoe manufacturer where 1,700 factory workers are organized in teams, employs only three managers. Traditionally, many workers did only what they were told to do and did not think beyond their own jobs. Under team structure, managers meet with hourly workers to decide daily quotas. Work teams then are given daily quotas; when the quotas are made, they are free to leave. Occasionally, special teams work on cross-functional projects. Such team structuring of work in this nonunion shop seems to work well for Vans, but it is far from the potential of union–management team planning that has been pioneered by a number of companies with strong unions.

Worker teams at General Motor's Saturn plant do more than assemble: they hire, approve parts from suppliers, choose equipment, and administer their budgets. Employees are involved in review of managers' performance. Saturn's UAW contract puts everyone on salary. Workers have a voice in all management decisions, and 20 percent of their pay hinges on quality, productivity, and profitability. At GM's traditionally managed divisions, both management and labor appear skeptical of such radical new ways now in place at Saturn and NUMMI, the joint GM-Toyota venture in Fremont, California. The new way is collaboration—which is teamwork.

A GE plastics plant had a long history of adversarialness. Management saw the union as blocking changes. The union saw management as a threat to union influence and to job security. Plant managers had been changed frequently, and some of them had made poor strategic decisions, such as the purchase of expensive machinery from Europe that could not be made to work. Funds were scarce to maintain older machines, which were producing the goods to keep the plant afloat. The work force had been cut by more than half.

The effort to move toward a team-organized work force was greeted with considerable "here we go again" skepticism. Team building in the plant lasted approximately a year and a half. During that period, week-long training team development seminars were conducted for work groups on all three shifts. Each seminar was composed of a mix of 25 to 40 line employees, engineers, maintenance, sales, staff, and management. During these sessions, there was plenty of ventilation of past and present gripes. But as the week progressed, the central training room walls were covered with reports from group deliberations in breakout rooms.

This plantwide team building was documented on videotape. In the first team training session, one especially conscientious engineer said that he felt that he was already part of a team and that he thought that the time and money for team training could be better spent elsewhere. It was not until after he was brought together with others in the plant that he said "I didn't realize that I worked with so many people that did not feel that they were part of a team."

One worker on a production line, who volunteered as part of spoilage team, found that others sneered at his efforts:

> When I went down to the press to talk to the operators, they told me, "You're on the *rat* team." I asked them what they meant. They said, "You're gonna go up there and rat on us and what we do." And I said, "No that's not what we're doing, we're looking mostly at mechanical things." I said, "We're not trying to put people in a hole, we're just trying to get the machines so they do right and to make sure people understand what they're supposed to do." So it was a good experience.

Skepticism gradually changed to cautious enthusiasm. The engineer who had thought the money could be better spent elsewhere said that during the past 16 months he had been a member of 8 different teams and the product they were putting out now "could go up against anyone in the world." Other workers talked about the "walls coming down" and now "having the courage to say, 'This does not meet our standards' rather than ship it out."

Basic Assumptions of the Team-Based Workplace

To explain team dynamics is to philosophize about human nature. Simple self-interest drives us to maximize the benefit for effort expended. But seeing individuals as solely motivated by self-interested survival instincts misses the broader understanding of human nature.

Humankind is also motivated by what Robbin Derry calls a collaborative self. It is the collaborative self that has enabled humankind to accomplish the complex tasks that are the products of organizational life. It is both the enlightened self-interest and the prompting of the collaborative self that inform us that the achievement of personal advantage involves helping others through a cooperative endeavor.

The team approach to achieving organizational goals, thus, feeds the motivations of both individual self-interest and the collaborative self. Teams give workers voice. In teams, both expression of job self-interest and collective interests are expected. In traditionally managed organizations, workers do not have a vehicle to talk constructively about their job concerns. Lacking the vehicle of work teams, employee communication is thwarted and, in turn, so is worker performance.

Maintenance of individual self-esteem and opportunity for self-actualization have a better chance in a team environment than in a Lone Ranger work terrain. This line of reasoning suggests that the possibility of peak performance is slim without a team approach to working life. A team-structured workplace in some ways is more difficult to organize than a traditional line-authority workplace. Democracy is the modus operandi of real teamness. Teams are a constructive vehicle for making workers' voices heard. When employee voice is mute, both workers' interests and quality of work suffer.

Democracy entails coping with differences of opinions, with discussion and debate. It is more time consuming and much more difficult to manage than a dictatorship. Democratic decision making takes more patience and sensitivity than handing down assignments, giving orders, and barking commands.

Charles Dygert, business consultant and author of *Success Is a Team Effort*, says that "the moment you make the transition from an autocratic to a democratic environment . . . you have introduced a new element into the game plan. It's called stress." Dygert explains that stress is different from the fear employees feel under a dictator boss, a fear that evolves into an "I don't give a damn" attitude and sometimes sabotage. Within a democratic work environment, the different stress experienced is the healthy tension that comes with a work ethic that entails sharing the load, collaboration, open resolution to differences of opinions, and creative ideas.

McKinsey & Company, the Cadillac of consulting firms, proposes that teams are most effective when they are aligned in a parallel manner, with each doing lots of steps in a process, rather than in a series with fewer steps. This permits employee rotation of tasks, cross-training, and seeing the product or service to completion. McKinsey's plan further recommends that each employee should develop several competencies, and team performance should be rewarded rather than individual performance alone.

Incidentally, McKinsey has had its difficulties. Seeds of greed sprouted internal discontent in the 1980s when a distinction was made between partners and directors. Some partners who left the firm say that the directors were given special perks such as occasional vacations with their wives whereas partners were sent stag to training meetings. The director's pay has soared above the partners, with the gap between the highest paid and the lowest paid being 50 to 1.

Teamwork is dangerous in that it fosters the notion that greed is bad and that fairness is good. Therefore, management should not expect much team spirit if it provides itself with privileges such as special parking places and air conditioned offices which production workers don't receive. Organizations that truly want teamwork will find that fairness and equity are basic.

In team-cultured companies, marketing, manufacturing, and finance departments are called on to work together. The reasoning behind this idea is that people with different business perspectives can put their heads together to solve a problem quickly and effectively. Members of a team must be accountable to the other members. They must work with the whole organization in mind rather than just their specific jobs.

Teamwork Centers in Process

Team organization is built around processes rather than specific tasks or separate departments. And communication, because it is a process, is an essential concern. Communication is a feed forward of messages. It is an encoding and a decoding interpretation of messages. It is questioning to learn exactly what is meant. It is feedback and double interact between sender and receiver. Teamwork is determined by how effectively messages are sent, interpreted, and responded to.

Think of some examples of how your boss and co-workers communicate.

Hierarchy is flattened by team structures around large processes. Managerial and nonmanagerial activities are combined to allow teams to take on tasks such as scheduling, hiring, and evaluating. Working with vendors is especially important to identifying how materials and just-in-time delivery can best meet a team's process needs. Customer contact is equally essential for team members to understand what the customers want. This often means trips to suppliers, meetings with customers, and sometimes joint problem-solving teams with suppliers and customers to find solutions that will give the work team what is needed and, in turn, will give customers what they want.

NONE OF US IS AS SMART AS ALL OF US.

Chapter Two

Highly Effective Teams

Sport teams often are micromanaged. In football, different coaches train offensive and defensive units, and there are special coaches for quarterback passing and receiver pairs. Coaches study game films and map out strategies in skull sessions. Players are there to listen and learn. On the field, coaches dictate plays, send in substitutions, and call time-outs. Players either follow instructions or are benched.

In the workplace, teamness has a number of practices in common with team sports as well as many ways in which they differ. Some work of team members is more individualistic, such as in tennis or golf; other work of teams is more improvisational, such as the ever-changing play in volleyball, soccer, and basketball; yet other work teams carefully devise game plans such as in football. Highly effective work teams learn what style of activity will best deliver their particular goods and services. Despite some variation in style, there are distinctive characteristics that highly effective work teams hold in common.

What characteristics make your work group distinctive?

Highly Effective Teams Alternate Skull Sessions and Action

Teamness at work is not a matter of following coaches' orders. Bosses can no longer micromanage performance. Teams at their best engage in a collaborative process of shared leadership and followership. That is what was meant by Robert Blake and Jane Mouton, who conceptualized interdependent work effort as 9,9 in their *The Managerial Grid*, when they likened effective teamwork to football:

> True team action is more like a football situation where division of effort is meshed into a single coordinated result; where the whole is more than the sum of its individual parts . . . Each person shoulders a different part of the total job, with each having 100 percent responsibility for success of the whole.

Highly Effective Teams Encourage Critical Involvement

Scholars of organizational dynamics are in agreement that employee involvement is high in effective teams. The senior researcher of the well-known Western Electric Hawthorne experiments in productivity, Elton Mayo, described the work units with whom his researchers worked:

> The group unquestionably develops a sense of participation in the critical determinations and becomes something of a social unit.

Highly Effective Teams Balance Individual and Group Worth

Douglas McGregor, who made Theory X and Theory Y famous to management schools in *The Human Side of Enterprise*, lamented:

> Most so-called management teams are not teams at all, but collections of individual relationships with a boss in which each individual is vying with every other for power, prestige, recognition, and personal autonomy. Under such conditions unity of purpose is a myth.

Rosabeth Moss Kanter, a former editor of the *Harvard Business Review* and principal in the Goodmeasure consulting firm, has been unable to talk about effective organizations without frequent use of the *team* word. In *The Change Masters* she wrote:

> "Individual" and "team" are not contradictory concepts in the innovating organization. Teams—whether in formal incarnations or as an implied emphasis on coalition formation and peer cooperation—are one of the integrative vehicles that keep power tools (information, resources, and support) accessible.

Highly Effective Teams Are Calmly Supportive

Rensis Likert, in describing what he referred to as System 4 Participative Management in *New Patterns of Management*, stated:

> The supportive atmosphere of the highly effective group stimulates creativity. The group does not demand narrow conformity as do the work groups under authoritarian leaders.

More recently, Robert Waterman, co-author of *In Search of Excellence*, when describing the core of calmness and lack of angst that typified successful management in *The Renewal Factor*, attributed successful management to teamness:

> Almost without exception, the successful people stress the importance of teamwork . . . Teamwork is a tricky business; it requires people to pull together toward shared goals or values. It does not mean that they always agree on the best way to get there. When they don't agree, they should discuss—even argue—those differences.

Waterman points out that when "teams-are-theory-in-use," communication is the way of finding and sorting out the best directions for an organization.

Highly Effective Teams Are Introspective about Process

The verdict is unanimous that effective teams take time to examine *how well they are doing*. Yale management professor Chris Argyris states that co-workers can recognize when they are functioning as a team through regular self-assessments. He employed tape recordings of manager–subordinate staff meetings to discover the signs of ineffective and effective groups. Signs of teamness can be evaluated by those who work together by comparing individual members' scores on the following 10 indicators suggested by Professor Argyris:

Signs of Teamness

Can't Say		Never					Always
?	Contributions are additive	0	1	2	3	4	5
?	Sense of team spirit	0	1	2	3	4	5
?	Decisions are made by consensus	0	1	2	3	4	5
?	Commitment to decisions is strong	0	1	2	3	4	5
?	Team continually evaluates itself	0	1	2	3	4	5
?	Team is clear about its goals	0	1	2	3	4	5
?	Conflict is dealt with openly	0	1	2	3	4	5
?	Alternative solutions are generated	0	1	2	3	4	5
?	Leadership goes to best qualified	0	1	2	3	4	5
?	Feelings are dealt with openly	0	1	2	3	4	5

This technique was effectively used in a BF Goodrich plastics plant. Work groups completed the Signs of Teamness before and after a six-month team building effort. Those pre- and posttest scores on each item were significantly different; in each case the average score was 2 to 3 points higher in the posttest.

Once a work group starts talking about how well it is communicating and performing, it is on the road to teamness. The shift to becoming a highly effective team is facilitated by a tool such as the Signs of Teamness. When it is *OK and expected* to talk about these signs, a sensitivity to working together improves. What does this tell us? The lesson is clear. Work groups can become teams—if and when—they work on communicating as a team.

What signs of teamness does your team illustrate?

Highly Effective Teams Are Attentive to Continuous Quality Improvement

Quality performance hinges on a work team's ability to define key input variables (KIVs) and key output variables (KOVs). In the traditionally managed workplace, employees are assigned to perform certain tasks, thus doing good work is following one's job description. "Just do it and don't ask why" is the standard operating procedure.

Effective teams, however, ask questions. They systematically diagram the variables that affect specifications (raw materials, time of delivery, on-site handling, machines, maintenance, workers' competence, workers' attitudes, supervisors' instructions). Effective teams are rigorous about specifications that the customers want and the product that is being shipped out.

The analytical problem-solving process entails sorting out the causes of wasted material and time and of out-of-spec output. It means measuring those variables that can be measured and monitoring those variables that are more intangible such as morale. This involves careful record keeping and special statistical analysis. Most of all, it means that those co-workers on the team must rigorously practice problem solving. Sometimes what is referred to as a fishbone diagram enables a team to **see** the KIVs and KOVs.

For example:

Each of the above six variables needs to be examined to learn what variable or what combination of variables may be causing the defect.

There are many ways to diagram the flow-through process from supplier to customer. This is a process that is applicable for both the external end customer and the internal interim customers (different work units) in the production sequence.

Suppliers————————Process————————Customer

Getting from input to output is a process that a team continuously examines. Skull sessions do not imply a coach diagramming team plays. Team skull sessions are heady meetings in which all members enter into the analysis of the process. They plan, they do, they check, they act. This chain of activity is a familiar sequence for highly effective teams.

The *plan-do-check-act* model is an application of scientific problem solving to the work place. This is a model that was proposed by the earliest quality gurus.

Plan is a time for locating and defining what is wasteful, what is defective and out of specifications, what is causing harm, what is less than excellent, and what is wanted by the customer that is not being delivered. Planning is a time to analyze the current system. Planning is a time to map out a trial solution. *Do* is a time to try out that improvement—to carry out on a small scale the specific trial. *Check* is a time to observe the effects of that improvement trial. It is a time to rigorously weigh the outcome of the trial—to discover if any negative side effects have come from the change. *Act* is a time to act on what was learned—to standardize the change if the change is for the good, and it is a time to search for other improvements. If not, the plan, do, check, and act pattern begins again.

Highly Effective Teams Are Passionate about Doing What Is Right

So often slogans about doing what is right center on production. Employees are told that doing wrong things right may be efficient but as stupid as doing right things wrong and doing wrong things wrong. Doing right things right is the cure for stupidity. Right things are defined as satisfying customers and retaining their loyalty. Such *right* talk makes one examine production practices, and that is good business.

What are some examples of "right talk" that your team uses?

But a passion for doing things right should mean much more. The quest for quality (i.e., efficiency and excellence) by highly effective teams is a moral matter. Ethical considerations permeate the concern for all workplace stakeholders: shareholders, management, workers, suppliers, distributors, customers, regulators, corporate neighbors, and the general public. Stakeholders are encouraged to voice their concerns.

Some companies create oversight teams—committees with representatives from the stakeholder groups—to act as the corporate conscience. Corporate responsibility committees can do much to raise attention to selfishness and greed. They can help prevent cost-saving shortcuts that are penny wise and pound foolish. They can celebrate commitment to integrity.

A passion for doing what is right revolves around what is good for customers, what is healthy for the stakeholders, and what is fair.

Chapter Three

From Quality Circles to Self-Directed Work Groups

The 100-acre San Diego Zoo is considered by many to be the number one zoo in the United States. In addition, the Zoological Society manages the 1,600 acre Wild Animal Park north of the city. These parks contain well over 5,000 animals. Five million visitors annually pass through their gates. The zoo generates $75 million yearly in revenue and employs 1,200 year-round workers. During the peak summer season, there are as many as 1,800 employees. Its newest exhibit "houses" the animals in bio-climatic zones.

Quality Circles

At the San Diego Zoo, quality circles started in the mid-1980s. David Glines, head of employee development, tells that the first QC was composed of union stewards. They were known as the Shop Stewards QC. Glines rose through the ranks as a night janitor and groundskeeper to become active as Teamsters Union Local 481 steward. The Teamsters is the union at the Zoo.

The work of that first QC effort led to a number of policy changes. Chief among them was the establishment of a Board of Justice to deal with grievances. That board heard 480 grievances, which represented a backlog of two years. It also won support for a plan in which zoo employees could "loan out" to another job that was temporarily open without risking loss of their current job.

The next step was to create a QC steering committee for the zoo. Since 1985 was the "Year of the Cat," the steering committee chose the acronym QCAT for Quality Circle Advisory Team. A similar team was created for the Wild Animal Park Circle Advisory Team (WAPCAT).

Glines trained 140 employees to be QC facilitators. QCs numbered as many as 30 at one point, but then dwindled to 15. QCs seemed to work better for the grounds department. The QC program had its ups and downs and reemerged in other forms of employee involvement such as:

- PRIDE (Personal Responsibility In Daily Effort): a low-cost employee recognition program developed by one circle and administered by employees.
- New exhibits co-planned by architects and employees who maintained them.
- An employee survey that involved employees at all levels in pursuit of excellence.

Glines believes that QCs were influential for changing a culture from autocratic to democratic. The old structure consisted of 50 departments. QCs laid the groundwork for autonomous work groups, a form of organization of work at the zoo that is especially suited to new projects.

Have you ever been involved in any quality circles? If so, how was it?

The Self-Directed Team

Tiger River Run is one such project that is managed by an autonomous seven-member team. Each department was asked to offer its best people for Tiger River. Team members, therefore, came from Building and Grounds, Horticulture, Birds, and Mammals. Rich J. Reese, an outside consultant, helped train and form the team in a series of workshops and planning sessions. At first, there were 11 members of the team, but when the members learned each other's skills, they found that the team could be cut to seven.

A unique aspect of the project was cross-training to do one another's jobs. Building and grounds attendants learned to cut food and animal keepers learned to wash windows. One team member tracks the display's budget on a personal computer. There is a sense of mutual responsibility and ownership for Tiger River that includes an aviary. Formal meetings are few. Decisions are made by consensus. Vacations and days off are negotiated.

Tiger River Run team members said, "Everyone here is happier and more productive . . . there is a better support system here than before the team" and "in the past two years there has been only one sick call. That says a lot for people wanting to come to work."

The way Tiger River Run and other similar autonomous teams are managing the bio-climatic zones, Glines predicted, will be the way almost all the zoo will be organized in the future. At the zoo, the future is now.

The Speak Up Generator

Changes at the San Diego Zoo can be traced to an organizationwide survey. The zoo's employee survey was carefully designed. Employees and top management were involved up front. Its name was wisely chosen—Voice: Speak Out for Action.

The Zoological Society's board of trustees and Director Doug Myers promised in a letter to all employees that survey findings would be "used by employees working together to improve operations as well as the quality of our daily work life." More specifically, Director Myers promised the survey would be anonymous, a summary of results would be shared with the whole society, and he was committed to action.

How can your work group improve the quality of your daily work life?

The Vital Follow Through

The employee steering committee was carefully selected. Its task was to set the goals and see to it that survey items addressed the goals. Managers were also involved and encouraged to allow paid time for employees to fill out the survey. *Voice* bulletins began in early 1987 to explain the process and prepare the employees for it. The first bulletin reiterated Myers' promises of anonymity, feedback, and action. It warned that one's say in the organization would die if not voiced by filling out the survey.

Survey results were disseminated quickly to employees. The April *Voice* bulletin presented a summary of survey findings in terms of "strengths and opportunities for improvement." In addition, some "high priority/quick win" actions were announced such as setting up an employee hotline, appointing a task force to study the uniform code, setting up meetings between the executive team and departments, publishing reports of the zoo's quality circle program, and scheduling quarterly management briefings.

An animal conditions task force (ACT) was formed. To become more visible, top executives made site visits according to a visit-a-job schedule. Uniform policy was modified to allow more options such as wearing panda, golden monkey, and zoo anniversary T-shirts. These were made available at half price.

ACT meetings were open to all interested parties. A number of simple but practical improvements were made as a result of the meetings. For example, "Watch Your Head" signs posted next to the boarding of the skyfari gondolas proved ineffective, so neoprene strips were installed.

Only when an employee survey is closely followed by action will it do more good than harm. David Glines, who oversaw the project, says the Speak Out for Action survey is a helpful tool. He promised a follow-up survey to see if employees believe that progress is being made.

See Chapter 34 for additional readings.

lower return to labor hours worked. The difference between traditional and transformational practices can be traced to improved dispute resolution and increased cooperation. This finding is particularly important. Why? Because if this difference is present for a plant in which union–management relations were quite good, an even greater difference should be the case in companies with more adversarial traditional labor–management relationships.

Does your organization more closely resemble a traditional or a transformational workplace? How does this orientation affect teamwork?

Xerox achieved the high honor of receiving the Malcolm Baldrige National Quality Award in 1989, but that is not the end of the story. During the waiting period in which the application was under preparation, many opportunities for improvement were identified. In anything but elegant language, it was declared in the company magazine, the *Benchmark*, that Xerox had "warts."

The Wart Report

The wart report listed 500 ugly problems, each of them pictured as a wart hog, and 50 recommendations were sent to top management. The wart report stressed that managers should manage from facts rather than manage by opinion, and that continuous improvement should be the goal rather than meeting standards. Killing off the wart hogs had begun.

Xerox's major manufacturing costs and defects were cut in half. Surveys of customer satisfaction veered upward by 38 percent, and Xerox recaptured the lead in moderately priced copiers. David Kearns, CEO during this period of revitalization, boasted that Xerox's competition for the quality award encompassed learning from other exceptional companies such as Milliken and Motorola. The copying—learning from others—process goes on. Benchmarking is copying in the best sense of the word.

Think of a few examples of how your team contributes to your organization's benchmarking process.

The symbolism entailed in Xerox's name for its company magazine, *Benchmark*, is rooted in the history of the term. Benchmarking refers to measuring one's work against the marks made on a workbench by the master craftsman. As a winner of the Malcolm Baldrige National Quality Award, Xerox is required to spread the word—to eagerly tell its story of quality improvement and serve as a benchmark that other companies may copy.

The Department of Labor, in its recent publication *High Performance Work Practices and Firm Performance*, encourages the copycat practice of benchmarking. This report also stresses that high performance firms involve employees in learning what the best-in-the-class teams are doing.

Does your organization encourage employee involvement in decision-making? How could you make your input count?

Chapter Four

The Benchmark Process

In 1959, Xerox sold its first plain-paper copier. Xerox once was a tiny corporation named Haloid located in Webster, New York, near Rochester. Since the beginning, Xerox has grown to employ 100,000 people and to control the worldwide share of the copier market. However, its story has not been one without major competition. Canon, Ricoh, Kodak, 3M, Minolta, Savin, Mita, Toshiba, Panasonic, Pitney Bowes, and Royal provided stiff competition. From a market share of 82 percent in 1976, Xerox's share plunged to 41 percent in 1982.

The story of how Xerox bounced back is exciting and is summed up in what is known as Team Xerox. The Amalgamated Clothing and Textile Workers Union (ACTWU) is the designated representative of some 4,000 employees in the main plant at Rochester. Except for one major strike, labor–management relations were relatively peaceful during the 1960s and 1970s. The relationship, although comparatively quiet, included much informal conflict resolution, some filing of formal grievances, and low levels of trust. Such a pattern is what Professor Joel Cutcher-Gershenfeld, who studied this plant over an extended period, refers to as traditional.

Turning Adversity into Aspiration

Trouble comes with layoffs. During 1981 and 1982, over 5,000 employees, including 1,200 union members, were laid off. This layoff, coupled with management's proposed subcontracting assembly of wire harnesses, strained the moderately peaceful labor–management relations. A series of union–management meetings were called. One outcome of those meetings was the formation of a joint task force to investigate if any viable alternatives might be found to prevent subcontracting. Ways were found. The task force came up with ways for 120 people to do the work of 200 and to provide new work for the remaining 80 workers.

The 1983 collective bargaining resulted in pivotal agreements. Management promised to suspend subcontracting and also guaranteed not to lay off any ACTWU members for three years. In exchange, the union conceded co-pay provisions for health care, no wage increase in the first year, and restriction on a no-fault absenteeism policy.

Thus began a transformation from low trust to union–management collaboration. That transformation evolved into genuine employee involvement in problem solving, information sharing, and autonomous decision making. Of course, some work groups are more transformational in attitude and in practice than others, and some remain more traditional in mind set and practice.

Transformational Climate

Professor Cutcher-Gershenfeld tracked 25 work units in the components manufacturing plant. For three years, he took monthly readings on frequency of conflicts, amount and quality of problem solving, changes in work design, and feedback transmitted on cost, quality, and schedule. These measures were then correlated with loss to scrap, defects, meeting schedule, and net return to hours worked. What did he find?

Work units with traditional practices as compared to work units with transformational practices had higher costs, more scrap, lower productivity, and a

Chapter Five

Understanding Team Dynamics

Because of the popularity of the T-word, many work groups call themselves a team long before they have earned that right. But it's no sin to want to be a team. The group dynamics that must take place before becoming a highly effective work team, if understood, can make the road to arriving at teamness more efficient and much less stressful.

Working in close relationship with others can be stressful. Special attention in this chapter, therefore, is paid to the interpersonal dynamics inherent in group interaction. The dynamics that we examine are inclusion, power, values, communication cycles, task tracks, relationship tracks, roles, phases, and creative problem-solving practices.

Inclusion

Sociologists speak of *in groups* and *out groups*. In organizational life, there are different degrees of in-ness and out-ness. Sometimes those who work at corporate headquarters feel that they belong to Company XYZ, whereas those who are employed at a distant site may feel that they belong to that local plant but are not really a part of the organization as a whole.

What are some signs of team belongingness?

Belonging to, being a member of, being in, and being accepted into are different ways of expressing the fundamental dynamic of inclusion in group life. Beginning a new assignment with any work unit starts the juices flowing—a nervous internal tension of wondering if one is accepted. This concern may subside after time, but membership and inclusion are continuous human concerns. In groups, indicators of inclusion are being on a membership roll, being encouraged to speak, being given jobs to do, and being asked to agree or disagree with items up for decision.

Power

Work groups are configured into subdivisions within an organizational structure. These groupings are at various levels within the hierarchy. Every group, because of who is in it, has a certain level of power and clout. Therefore, some groups may feel that they are in the loop of making things happen, and others may feel they are out of the loop. Every work group is concerned about its relationships with other groups and with those managers who are upward in the firm's hierarchy.

Power is a fundamental consideration in the formation of any new group. Sport team managers and scouts want to recruit members who have the talents to fill the varied positions needed, but whatever the kind of team, they want to be sure to recruit power players. Likewise, in work teams, power hitters matter. These are the individuals who have special technical expertise and special influence.

Individuals within a group inevitably experience the same power concerns that their work group has with the organization. Each individual silently asks her- or himself, "Where do I rank in this group?" That question is partially answered by seeing who emerges as a leader of the work group. Obviously someone who is appointed as leader or is voted by the work group to serve as the spokesperson will feel more *up* than down. Those who rarely get to express their opinions will usually feel *down*. The up or down feeling is a matter of power within the group.

What makes a work team different from a work group, other than its size, is that a team shares leadership. This does not mean that all individuals are equally talented technically or equally able to serve as a spokesperson. But it does mean that there is a special sensitivity to sharing power. This shared power shows up in turn taking in communication, in performing tasks, and in having an equal say in decisions.

Does your work group share leadership?

Values

Individuals hold certain beliefs and strong preferences. They bring these beliefs and strong preferences into the work group. When individuals work at individual assignments, these beliefs and preferences for the most part are hidden. This is not the case when one is in a group. Americans value the virtues of individualism—an ethic of hard work and sacrifice. Most believe that idleness is a sin, industry is valued, and those people who are poor are more than less to blame for their condition.

Americans celebrate material accumulation and financial success. Property and possessions cannot be protected without law and order and a strong defense. Each individual must fight for herself or himself. Life goes to the survival of the fittest.

Counter to individualism is a concept called friendly world identity. Those who value a friendly world, as opposed to an individual work ethic, want life to be less impersonal. They treasure ideas more than material possessions. Freedom of speech and having a say in one's workplace and community are as equally important as law and order. Status receives less respect than equality.

Obviously, when people bring varying degrees of individualism and friendly world values into a work group, there is a clash of wills. As work groups evolve into teams, these values will surface. Teams will talk out differences as they relate to their work. Sometimes these values will be compromised or negotiated. At other times the conflicting values will be avoided. Naturally, people will be attracted to others within their work group whose values are similar. *Close* and *far* are words that describe the feelings of more or less liking for certain others in one's work group or for one's group as a whole.

Communication Cycles

Interaction in a group is more than turn taking. Communication consists of two types of agendas: one that is visible and one that is hidden. The visible agenda follows subjects that the group or leader brings to discussion. An agenda for a manager's group might be problems pertaining to pricing and distribution of goods and services. An agenda provides structure for communication and helps resolve the question of "What are we supposed to do?" Groups that are not accustomed to deliberating together often wonder and wander around that question. Learning to collectively deal with a topic such as continuous quality improvement is far different from following orders.

A hidden agenda consists of topics and goals that are not voiced. A supervisor meeting with a work group may want to stop bad mouthing the engineers and management, but rather than deal with the topic, the supervisor suggests that being professional should be on the agenda.

Group communication usually focuses on tasks. However, perhaps even more important (although rarely a topic on the agenda), there is communication about relationships. The frustrations and tensions that revolve around getting a task accomplished often concern people differences about what should be done, people resistance to change, and people failure to be responsible.

The Task Track

The *task track* for a group generally entails sequential interaction on the following themes:

- Leadership/membership decisions.
- Dissatisfactions and/or desires expressed.
- Proposals debated/decided.
- Mission assigned.
- Discussion of how the group will be viewed and how it might have favorable public image.
- A review of its performance.

These topics are not always announced on the agenda, and often they are not all dealt with at one session. But these are the concerns of a work group that is evolving into a team.

Highly effective teams will develop patterns, traditions, and habits of procedures that sociologists call norms. Highly effective teams encourage differences of opinions. Highly effective groups rarely vote to resolve differences. Rather, they confer until there is a tentative agreement, or at least no strong objection to a course of action.

What norms has your work group developed?

The process of gaining general agreement is called decision by consensus. Operating by consensus requires sensitivity to one another. Team members need to check with each other to determine if general agreement exists. This checking is not always done by the leader. In effective teams, each person shares the responsibility for a quick check to learn if everyone is willing to go along with a decision. Effective communication entails periodic recaps of what has been agreed on. Posting these points of agreement on newsprint proves to be a time-saving practice.

Working by consensus, however, does not mean careless agreement to what is being said. On the contrary, highly effective teams are rigorous in:

- Describing symptoms of a problem.
- Locating and analyzing causes of a problem.
- Generating possible solutions to a problem.
- Debating the pros, the cons, and the negative consequences of potential solutions.
- Implementing and testing a solution that appears worthwhile.
- Evaluating the trial.

The Relationship Track

Communication about relationships within a group usually occurs after meetings by two or more of the group's members. These after-meeting conversations arise because of feelings about how well or how poorly the group worked together. These feelings pertain to such interpersonal variables as liking and disliking each other, domination and withdrawal among members, and willingness and unwillingness to do one's share of the work.

Distress is keenly felt when some team members feel they are being treated unfairly. Work teams want to be treated fairly by other work teams and by their superiors. They want their team effort to be rewarded. The reason for teamwork rather than individual work assignments is that teamwork can produce more effectively than can individuals. Teams are teams because they are more rewarding.

In similar fashion, each individual member of a team wants the effort he or she puts into the team's work to be rewarded. Individuals want their effort to be maximally rewarding. In short, each of us wants what we give to match what we get. If some co-workers on the team are not carrying their load but are receiving the same rewards, that seems unfair. If some team members are getting the choice assignments, that seems unfair. If some team members are dominating the discussion and decision making, that seems unfair.

Highly effective teams know that relationship tensions occur, and talking about feelings sometimes is more important than talking about tasks. Highly effective teams, therefore, set aside time to talk about how they feel and whether anyone is listening to their opinions. Relationship tension sometimes is linked to the communication roles that we play.

Roles

Communication roles in task accomplishment (in goal setting, problem solving, and continuous quality improvement) include:

- Getting things started, contributing ideas, asking questions, and contributing information.
- Elaborating, clarifying, sometimes blocking, and rigorously testing information for factual authenticity, and weighing the potential negative consequences of a proposal.
- Seeking compromise, summarizing, helping the group to be sensitive to fair procedures, and checking for consensus.

Communication scholars have learned that task accomplishment of a group progresses in a reach-test spiral. This means that a co-worker's comment is reacted to by one or more co-workers, and then the first person replies to the responses. A group will discuss an idea that has been put forth until there is general agreement or rejection of it. Agreement or rejection depends upon how well the idea is found to fit the facts and values of the group. Once there is consensus on an idea, someone will reach for another idea, and the reach-test spiral will begin again.

Words are ambiguous by nature. They have different meanings to different people. Coming to agreement about what is intended is a two-way process. This suggests that communication within a group is immensely complex because more than two people must come to an understanding about what is meant. It is a process that entails dealing with messages that require some interpretation before they are assembled into configurations of meaning that are acceptable, retained, and built upon.

To facilitate group communication, various individuals of a team will play relationship roles. These include:

- Feeling sensitive, one who encourages the less vocal to ask questions and give their opinions and one who seeks to keep the contribution turn taking balanced.
- Harmonizer, joker, clown, or tension reliever.
- Cheerleader or morale booster.
- Satisfaction tester, one who encourages the team to ask and evaluate how well it is working together.

The uniqueness of work teams is in many ways similar to a jazz group. Each member of a jazz combo may be especially good on a certain instrument and will take turns playing the lead roles. At other times, members of the group will play different instruments. Jazz groups play variations on a theme, and at times, they improvise. They take turns leading and following each other's lead.

Co-workers on a team usually are there because they have special expertise at certain positions or machines, but work teams usually cross-train, so that team members can do each other's jobs. Often, they rotate jobs. This practice serves the individual well in that it lessens repetitive motion injuries and boredom. It also serves the team well in that more than one individual is skilled should someone be injured or absent.

Communication roles of work team members also vary. Roles can be seen in three broad categories: communication pertaining to task accomplishment, communication pertaining to team relationships, and communication pertaining to self-interest. Individuals on a work team, just as in a jazz group, may play more than one role and one role more than others. Sometimes they may lead and other times they may follow. Still, they may play a different role or a combination of roles at different times.

Self-interest roles are expressed by communication that is directed more at personal advantage and attention getting than for the good of the team. These include:

- Grandstanding, star, prima donna, and interrupting behaviors.
- Verbal aggressiveness, boasting, criticizing, threatening, and verbal abuse that discounts the value of others.
- Blocking to the extent that consensus and even clarification of differences is impossible.
- Withdrawal, not following through on assignments, and not doing one's fair share.

After a while, teams will not tolerate excessive self-interested communication, and such behavior will be shut out. Team members who overact self-interested roles will be told to "shape up or ship out." Groups either confirm or reject roles by the way they respond to their members' communication.

Is your work group a team? If so, what roles are played by your team members? Include task accomplishment, relationship, and self-interest roles.

Phases

Some scholars of group dynamics say that groups typically evolve along predictable phases. Other scholars argue that group processes are difficult to predict. Phases most often mentioned are *orientation, conflict, emergence,* and *reinforcement*. Groups that experience some success often do experience the four phases. Unsuccessful groups may not get past the conflict phase. Groups take time to develop their habits and rules. There is a learning about one another, an orientation that occurs. Orientation is also necessary to reach agreement about what we are supposed to do. Conflict regarding goals, leadership, problem analysis, solution selection, and implementation does not take long to surface. Emergence is when conflict is sufficiently resolved and the group agrees .on certain solutions. Agreement is then reinforced by expressions of cohesiveness and endorsement of the solutions. The phases of orientation and conflict tend to recur each time a group convenes, but to a lesser extent as a group progresses into an emergence phase.

> *Think of an example of how your work group has gone through the four phases of orientation, conflict, emergence, and reinforcement.*

Perhaps the most frequently used description of phase development in groups is *forming, storming, norming,* and *performing*. People are miserable who fail to realize that conflict is the rule rather than the exception. Those, who by nature are introverts and cannot tolerate conflict and ambiguity, will find working in groups frustrating.

Groups that become teams will experience the difficult phases of group dynamics, but they will increasingly develop habits and procedures that result in effective problem solving.

Creative Problem-Solving Practices

Effective teams follow the rules of individual and team brainstorming: The green light is on. During idea generation, critical remarks are taboo. Free wheeling and hitchhiking are encouraged. Quantity of solutions is sought; the more the better. Follow-up sessions are then scheduled to sift out the ideas and solutions that have possibility.

Chapter Six

Before Team Training—
The Go/No Go Decision

Professional sports is a $70 billion business. In 1983, the Boston Celtics' franchise was purchased for $18 million. Today its selling price is at least $200 million. Ticket prices for a good seat are as much as $50. The professional management teams' duties include financial matters, recruitment of players, negotiation with unions, employment of crews for grounds and stadiums, ticket sales, vendors, media, and making travel arrangements for the club.

In the sport of football, there are generalist coaches and specialist coaches. Generalist coaches work with the offensive and defensive squads, and specialist coaches develop quarterbacks, linebackers, kickers, and receivers. Players are expected to jump on command. Players, regardless of their positions, are expected to know the game plan, to drill the plays into habits, and to respond in sync to those who call them. These various individual and team specialists are ordered into a game as needed.

The success of the organization depends on every work group functioning as part of the whole. Some of these work groups within the organization function as closely managed, whereas others function as semi-autonomous units. Yet, others function as self-directed teams. Spring training is not the same for everyone in the organization.

In what ways is your workplace similar to a professional football organization?

Large Team Configurations

Work practices can be categorized into three basic types: structural (job design, teamwork), human resources (training, communication), and technological (computerization, robotics). A synopsis of hundreds of studies is available from the U.S. Department of Labor, substantiating the fact that corporate America is eagerly experimenting with high-performance work practices. A few examples of large team configurations include Chrysler, New United Motor Manufacturing, and Rubbermaid.

When Chrysler sets out to create a new car or revamp an old one, Chrysler forms a "self-contained, multidisciplinary group" of 700 people, which includes teams of engineering, design, manufacturing, marketing, and finance specialists. Management puts forth contractual goals for this large team and then turns it loose. CEO Bob Eaton has declared top management at Chrysler does not micromanage its cross-functional teams. He explains the company's success in one word—empowerment.

The New United Motor Manufacturing Inc. (NUMMI) in Fremont, California, is a joint venture of Toyota, General Motors, and the United Auto Workers. Before this joint venture, General Motors and the UAW had a history of hostility and poor product quality. Since 1984, however, the plant has become a startling example of collaboration and turnaround in quality. Absenteeism is low. Car quality is high. Trust between management and the union is strong. Some 2,500 people are organized into self-directed work teams of 4–6 members. Each team has a team leader who reports to a group leader. Each team regularly coordinates the team's effort but does not engage in discipline. Teams decide on their own personnel and their own work procedures.

Year after year, *Fortune*'s survey listing the most and least admired companies finds that those at the top have strong cultures. Rubbermaid, for example, which garnered the number one spot two years in a row, relegates decision making to its several divisions, which are further decentralized into cross-functional teams. Each unit has its own design, research, and manufacturing staffs. CEO Wolfgang Schmitt boasts, "Our business teams are as nimble as entrepreneurs. The teams can reach anywhere in the company for resources."

Project Teams

Teamwork in the most admired organizations sometimes crosses company boundaries. For example, Motorola created a team of its sales and logistics group, a Motorola distributor, and a customer organization in an effort to shorten delivery time. As a result, this team shortened delivery time from 50 days to less than 24 hours.

Business is redrawing its boundaries. Changes are often restructured around projects rather than positions. Project work, in contrast to position-based work, has been the rule for years in industries such as construction, film making and television, and professional services. Within organizations, temporary project teams made up of core employees are increasingly used. But few organizations do everything in house. Contracting out project work is now common practice in most organizations. Project managers buy or lease facilities, capital, and people from resource providers. People employed for project work must function as project teams.

Cultural Readiness

Organizations are resistant to change. Chains of authority, policies, roles, rules, and regulations compose the structure of any organization. Almost everything about an organization conspires to make ways of thinking and doing taken for granted, or at least predictable.

Motivation for change usually comes from some downturn in profits or crisis in public confidence. That is what happened with the American auto industry. When Ford felt the pinch of global competition in 1979, it signed a contractual agreement with the United Auto Workers endorsing employee involvement. This agreement did not have an immediate payoff. It took years to uproot Henry Ford's assembly-line mind set, of only wanting to hire "a pair of hands."

To encourage employee commitment to the phrase "At Ford Quality is Job #1," a large-scale change strategy was undertaken. Week-long seminars with management promoted participative skills at all levels and within natural work groups. Gary Jusela was part of that large-scale change. In 1987, he moved to Boeing and was charged with accomplishing a similar cultural shift. Boeing's situation was far different from the trouble besetting Ford. Rather than feeling the pinch of global competition, Boeing was awash with billions of dollars in back orders. Boeing's balance sheet was spectacular, and its future looked even better.

Jusela found a way to sell management's concern for continuous quality improvement by using the metaphor of *arthritis*. Arthritis is a painful rigidity that often comes with maturity and aging, preventing certain parts from working smoothly with other parts. If his aging metaphor did not get Boeing workers' attention, competitors' threats would. One in-plant memo to all employees quoted the CEO of British Aerospace as saying, "Airbus is going to attack the Americans, including Boeing, until they bleed and scream." He also circulated letters from Japanese and European CEOs criticizing Boeing's poor quality and failure to deliver planes on schedule. Tragic news of a Boeing-built 737 coming apart over Hawaii made the arthritis warning persuasive and added substance to Jusela's arthritis metaphor.

Jusela also shared with the workers success stories of quality efforts in some work groups. The sheet metal fabrication division had its efforts captured on video. This included an off-site meeting with workers enthusiastically responding to teamwork. Some 4,000 ideas and suggestions were generated by that division. Suggestions included cross-training, day care for workers' children, and four 10-hour rather than five 8-hour work days. However, the idea that got the biggest vote was for employee stock options.

Yet in its push for continuous quality improvement, Boeing remained farsighted. One of Boeing's problems dated back to its 747, which was first put into service in 1970. The 747 had five fatal crashes in that decade, three of which were blamed on pilot error. Additionally, cracks were found in the engine mount pins and new and stronger ones were designed, but later they were also found to crack and suffer from corrosion. In the early 1990s, 747s crashed in Taiwan, Amsterdam, and Anchorage. In 1993, a Boeing team of engineers fixed the problem with a new stainless steel pin and a V-shaped brace.

On the wall of a Boeing office hangs a photo of a plane crash with this quotation: "Aviation in itself is not inherently dangerous, but to an even greater degree than the sea, it is terribly unforgiving of any carelessness, incapacity, or neglect." This account emphasizes that corporate culture dare not be complacent regardless of organizational financial success or failure.

Feasibility of Implementing Teams

During the decade of the 1980s when business was enamored with strong corporate culture, the joke was passed around about one chief executive who was reported to say, "Order us some of that strong corporate culture stuff." Just as worker commitment cannot be ordered, begged, or borrowed, an organizational culture must be receptive to change before team building and team training will be worth the effort.

We hear so much about the team way for today's workplace that we may assume that everyone needs team training. But before you embark on team training, pivotal questions must be addressed such as, Why do we need to have teams? Before *team* becomes a bitter word, careful planning must occur. A management announcement that "Henceforth, teams will be the way we do things!" will backfire if a corporate culture is not ready for teams.

How do you determine if you need to form a team in your organization? What are the primary decisions that must be made? Who should undertake development of teams? Do we need to survey employees about the feasibility of creating teams? Time invested addressing these questions will be well spent because a feasibility study team often evolves into a steering committee for organizational change. A feasibility team addresses what, who, and how questions.

What? The decision to *go team or no go team* is part of the larger questions posed near the beginning of this chapter:

- What work design and processes can best meet the mission of a particular work unit and the organization?
- What work configurations are appropriate to the corporate culture of a particular organization?

These are questions that merit periodic study. They are questions pertaining to safety, cost cutting, profitability, and customer and constituent confidence.

In addition, specific questions relating to the available technology and skills of various work units must be addressed.

- What are the most appropriate work configurations for particular tasks and people?
- How well are different work units functioning interdependently?

Who? When you have a small work group, all persons should be included in determining the feasibility of teams. But often work groups are part of a system, and, therefore, all levels of the organization must be involved in the feasibility study. Various levels of the organization might include its internal and external suppliers, its internal and external customers, its own and adjacent work groups' technology and space, and management. No matter how big or small your team may be, a feasibility study is an important task.

To determine who should be part of a feasibility study committee, a north, south, east, west model can be used. North includes the top executives and possibly representatives of major stockholders or owners. South includes a cross-section of production, staff, and service personnel. East is represented by suppliers, customers, and union members. West representatives might come from outside parties such as government and community.

How? Data can be gathered in various ways. For example, focus groups can provide early feedback on whether further data collection will do more harm than good. It is better not to ask questions that will arouse expectations of team processes if those who manage or if those employed are committed to autocratic traditions. If preliminary inquiries bring a modest to favorable go-for-it response, then additional data collection is merited through interviews, visits to benchmark organizations, and employee and customer surveys. We recommend that outside consultants be employed for an organizationwide feasibility study. Consultants have special expertise in collecting data, interpreting the results, and sharing the results with members of the organization.

Is it go team or no go? Major resistance to the study itself signals no go. Workers who do not want more say, do not want to bother with collaboration with other work groups, or dislike each other are not ready for teamwork. There may be more pressing needs such as equipment repair, problems with suppliers, distribution, or pay. A feasibility study is a time for testing if the shapers and shakers understand the pros and cons of team work configurations.

Go for it. Managers hunger for answers in turbulent times. Their jobs hinge on a quick fix to production and delivery problems. It is a disservice for team building to be sold as a quick fix; however, neither should team building be undersold. A feasibility study raises anxiety in an organization, therefore, it should not be kept under wraps. Rather, it should be an integral component of a corporate culture that embraces learning about better ways. A feasibility study is not simply an either go-team-or-no-go issue; rather, it is a more general study of how a workplace might continuously improve quality and become a high-performance, world-class organization.

Team Awareness

Members of an organization, no matter what level, want to and have a right to know what is going on. Therefore, a go-team decision should be one that emerges from an informed workforce. Workers should not be asked to buy into organizational change without awareness of the costs and benefits of teamness.

So what does a team awareness campaign entail?

1. It means corporatewide feedback of the data gathered by the feasibility study.
2. It means setting forth the scope of a change—where it will be tried, by whom, for what period, and how it will be evaluated.
3. It means educating those involved about what to expect from team building and team training. Several communication channels can be used to keep the workforce informed.

In two words, a team awareness campaign provides information and inspiration.

Remember the San Diego Zoological Society? In a letter to all employees, director Doug Myers promised that its Speak Out for Action survey would be used "by employees working together to improve operations as well as the quality of our daily work life." Prior to the survey's administration, in the zoo's *Voice* newsletter, Myers strongly urged employees to participate in the survey. He also pledged to turn its findings back soon. He promised to take quick action for changes where he could and to study those that would take more time. Those promises were kept. Survey findings were published in *Voice* and action committees were quickly formed to address a variety of concerns. The careful attention to what might be called an awareness campaign was a prelude to the experiments with semi-autonomous and self-directed bio-climatic teams.

People need to know that teamwork, as compared to individualized work, can be confusing and that conflict sometimes occurs after a short honeymoon. They need to know there is a transition period between seeking and finding the right kind of team for particular jobs. Managers should expect a period of ventilation if employees have not had open channels for voice. Workers need to know that sometimes superiors are not receptive to assertive voices. An awareness campaign can benefit from sending delegates to benchmark organizations engaging in various work systems.

An essential aspect of a team awareness campaign is to talk about boundaries. Workers should expect that changing from chains of command to team-managed work will not exempt them from the rigors of record keeping and the nitty-gritty budget keeping that management has previously shouldered. Workers also need to expect that it will take time to learn which kind of teams will work best within and among different work units. And they need to know that teams must work out rules of who is accountable for what.

Steering Committee, Team Building, and Team Training

A steering committee should be an expansion of an organization's management group. It is important, however, that a change effort not be a management mandate. This suggests that how a change effort is labeled will matter to employees. For example, *total quality management* might best be conceived and phrased as a *collaborative quality effort*.

Members of a feasibility study group are the natural leaders of a go-team-building steering committee. But it is important that new blood be brought into the leadership of organizational change. Therefore, a simple democratic process should be created for electing and rotating its membership. During its early stages, a steering committee's decisions should be tentative and experimental.

Team building differs from team training. Team building is site specific. Team training, we believe, is most effective if it is designed for natural work groups that compose a particular workplace. Bringing together co-workers, office staff, engineers, supervisors, managers, and sales personnel to work on specific needs can be an exhilarating work experience. Synergy is born in such team-building and team-training efforts.

Team building, when linked to team training, has special meaning. Teams form according to particular problems, such as spoilage problems, supplier problems, cycle reduction time, packaging, and so on. Teams develop in light of emerging leadership. Learning to share responsibilities is part of that process: deciding who does what, when, and where.

A self-directed work team, self-managing team, high-performance work group—whatever the label—generally is a group of 5 to 15 employees who are responsible for a whole product or process. The team plans the work and does it. Meeting time is set aside each week or day to set goals, give performance feedback, hire, and fire. As skills are mastered, the team grows in its responsibilities and confidence. Responsibilities can include coordination with other departments, keeping records, budgeting, and statistical process control. Most of all, the team seeks continuous quality improvement.

Team-building training of natural work groups, therefore, prepares a team to work out what tasks are to be performed by anyone of them who is available, what tasks should be performed by a team leader, what tasks should be left to a team facilitator or manager, and what tasks should not be done by anyone. Each natural work group determines what cross-training is needed and determines its administrative duties pertaining to budget, reports, discipline, and organizational regulations.

Generic team training for strangers from different work groups and workplaces, however, can have some benefits that site-specific natural work group team training may miss. Strangers, because they are free from a history of past work relationships, are freer to use new interpersonal and problem-solving skills. Generic team training can include systems' awareness, seeing the big picture, human relations skills, constructive role behaviors, problem-solving techniques, statistical process control, accountability procedures, and group communication skills.

Part II of this handbook presents many experiential team-building and training workouts. They are designed for either site-specific organizations that are in the process of developing a go-for-it team-building decision or generic teams.

These first six chapters have provided you with a picture of what it means to work as a team. We have tried not to oversell the benefits of teamwork. Making a team work well together requires both knowing what dynamics to expect and developing the attitudes and communication skills essential for successful group interaction. You now have the basics of what the experts have learned about how work groups function. You have read about workplacewide team building and the steps to take before team training. But book knowledge is not real know-how.

Knowing how to do something comes with doing. Part II, which follows, is the heart pounding and body building of this book. It contains instructions for team workout activity. These workouts provide you with opportunities to build team muscles—for making you more flexible, stronger, and wiser. That cannot happen by sitting in the bleachers and merely watching. Learning how to work as a team takes practice, practice, and more practice.

PART II
EXPERIENTIAL WORKOUTS FOR TEAM BUILDING

Chapter Seven

Note to the Trainer-Facilitator: How to Use Part II

This section was designed especially for you, the trainer-facilitator, and those enrolled in your training seminars or courses. After each essay is a workout that illustrates the key concept(s) of the essay. The exercises were written with you in mind, and we welcome the opportunity to discuss the approach you might take when using these exercises. We recommend that the trainer-facilitator who leads a workout first read the preceding essay. In some cases, the trainer-facilitator may wish to allot some seminar time to allow the participants to read the essay as well.

By now, we imagine that those of you with less experience as trainers are feeling a range of emotions. Perhaps you are nervous, scared, excited, or anxious—in any case, your feelings are not unusual. As trainers and facilitators ourselves, we know what you are experiencing. Whether you have led a team exercise before, the main thing is to relax! Take a deep breath, and enjoy the experience.

We urge you to take a close look at Figure 7–1, The Experiential Circle of Meaning. As a trainer-facilitator, you will be working with a group of people unique in their demands and requests. Not every participant in an exercise will demand the same treatment or explanation, but as a facilitator, you must expect the unexpected.

This model will help you in two ways. First, it allows you to adjust for and assume what will happen ahead of time. Second, it helps you anticipate questions or explanations the participants may ask or require.

The model begins with the participants engaging in an activity, either real or simulated. After the activity has been accomplished, you will need to (*a*) elicit a verbal description of what has happened, (*b*) share the thoughts and feelings of the participants as they went through the activity, and (*c*) interpret the significance of the activity as it relates to the participants' past experience and knowledge of life. At the end of each exercise, we have provided debriefing questions that can be used to facilitate group discussion. We recommend that as you first use these exercises, you follow the debriefing questions. As you become more adept at facilitating, feel free to improvise accordingly.

It is also important to stress the application of the training event to the participants' present and future work life. On the surface, some of these workouts may appear as fun and enjoyable. They are. We make no apology. But it is essential that the trainer facilitate before, during, and after a workout lest the participants fail to grasp its significance. This may involve a trial testing of the applications. After the workout has been completed, the participants will take the experience with them into any future encounter.

So there you have it! Have fun, enjoy yourself, but be aware of the responsibility that goes along with this task. A note of caution: Make sure that you are familiar with any exercise before you use it. Read the preceding essay, and if that is not enough, refer to the resources that we have placed at the back of

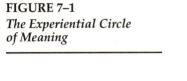

FIGURE 7–1
The Experiential Circle of Meaning

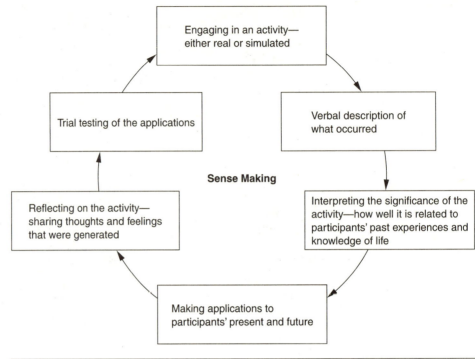

this book. A list of the materials that you will need for all the exercises is provided in Table 7–1. As trainers ourselves, we are all too aware of the pitfalls that occur because of not being knowledgeable about the exercise.

Probably the biggest mistake a trainer-facilitator can make is *not* repeating a workout. As we stressed in Chapter Six, know-how comes by practice, practice, and more practice.

Teamwork training can benefit three different kinds of seminar participants: strangers, members from different work groups within the same organization, and members of natural work groups. It is the natural work group that will benefit the most by engaging in the various workouts. These benefits include:

- Working on real work tasks.
- Having the opportunity to clarify dysfunctional work patterns.
- Generating team spirit.

But whether the participants are strangers or natural work groups, we know that you will enjoy the workouts—and that is the best possible climate for skills development.

Good luck!!

TABLE 7-1
List of Materials Needed for the Workout Exercises

General Materials Needed

  Paper and notepads
  Pens and pencils
  Flipchart
  Newsprint pad
  Colored markers
  Notecards, both 3" x 5" and 4" x 6" (some prepared in advance)
  Scissors
  Masking tape
  Award ribbons
  Large sheets of white paper

Specific Materials Needed

  Puzzle and pieces for "Piecing It Together"
  Gamepiece for "Rain, Rain, Go Away"
  Toy building blocks for "Go(al) Ahead"
  Pieces of rope for "Do Not Cross"
  Dominos for "Dominos and Interdependence"
  Set of small objects for "Get All You Can"

THE BIG PICTURE

Chapter 8   How Is Our Workplace a System?
Chapter 9   How Does Our System Operate?
Chapter 10 We're All in This Together
Chapter 11 And Now for the Weather…
Chapter 12 Uncommon Sense

THE BIG PICTURE

Chapter 8   How Is Our Workplace a System?
Chapter 9   How Does Our System Operate?
Chapter 10 We're All in This Together
Chapter 11 And Now for the Weather…
Chapter 12 Uncommon Sense

Chapter Eight

How Is Our Workplace a System?

If you were asked to define your workplace in a few words, how would you? Would you describe your job duties? Perhaps your co-workers? What about the clients that your organization serves? Or your personal feelings toward the organization? Regardless of your response, the relevant issue is that your response would be based upon how you view your organization operating as a system.

But what is a system, and how does a system work? A *system* can ideally be defined as "a set of interdependent units which work together to adapt to a changing environment." What this really means is that a system consists of elements that rely upon one another in order to function. Communication is the glue that holds the system together.

In order to fully understand how the workplace can be viewed as a system, we need to look at the elements that a system comprises. These elements include objects, attributes, relationships, and environments. As we go through the list, keep your organization in mind so that you can identify the specific elements that compose your system.

Objects are the units of a system—namely, the people who make up the organization. Without people, the system could not operate. Think of the people in your workplace. This includes everyone in the organization, not just those with a title or a fancy office. Sometimes we recognize only the people with whom we work, so it can be difficult for us to realize that *all* the people working in our organization are responsible for its functioning. In addition, we also have a tendency to forget that those people who do not work in the same physical setting as we are also part of the organization—for example, those individuals who may work in a different building or even in a different city. We need to remember everybody, because without them, we will be unable to function as a team.

Attributes are the qualities or characteristics of the objects. In this sense, we have to consider that every person in our organization has two sets of attributes: individual attributes, which consist of physical and personality traits, and organizational attributes, which define our job duties and responsibilities. Sometimes we only focus on a co-worker's personal attributes. But remember that organizational attributes are just as important. As organizational employees, we could easily identify some of our physical or personality traits—but in terms of the workplace, we can also identify some of our organizational attributes—"we are responsible for writing this essay" and "everyone must contribute a fair share to the work group." For the system to function efficiently, it is important that these attributes be defined so that all objects are aware of them. This idea also holds true for a team. Knowing *who* is part of the team and knowing *about* who is part of the team are two different concepts. In this sense, we need to know everything about our teammates.

Relationships are an essential part of any system. As we all know, most of our interpersonal relationships are a result of our own choice—we choose with whom we want to communicate. Unfortunately, our relationships at work may be more rigidly defined. But again, these are related to the smooth functioning of the organization, so we can't always pick and choose with whom we would like to interact. Yet, this does not have to be viewed as negative.

But do we always know about these relationships at work? While it may be easier to identify your interpersonal relationships outside of your work unit, a relatively easy way to do it at work is to look at your organizational chart. The chart should illustrate the relationships among work groups that result as a function of your organization. Keep in mind, though, that some relationships are not marked, such as a team. It is up to us to define the relationships that allow our team to communicate in the most productive way.

Interaction with the environment is required for your organization to survive. The *environment* can be defined as a suprasystem, in which your system coexists with other systems. Think how, on a daily basis, your organization is affected by systems around you—other organizations, clients, possibly other teams. For example, the political environment, which would include the local, state, and federal government, requires an organization to follow equal employment opportunity laws. By not being aware of other agencies and organizations, your organization could get in trouble as well as any other system that is part of the environment.

As you can see, your organization can be viewed as a system. A system consists of four elements: objects, attributes, relationships, and interaction within a larger environment. For an organization to function effectively, the system must take into account these elements and be able to identify them. This will allow the objects of the system to engage in successful team building.

See the Chapter Thirty Philadelphia Textile Mill study for an example of the consequences of not recognizing the organization as a system.

WORKOUT: WHAT IS A SYSTEM?

Purpose:	To acquaint participants with the elements of a system within their specific organization.
Group Size:	Any number.
Time Required:	45 to 50 minutes.
Materials:	Paper, pencils, markers, newsprint.
Seating Arrangement:	No preference.
Other Considerations:	None.
Process:	1. The trainer-facilitator gives each participant a piece of paper and instructs the participants to fold the paper in half twice, so that there are four squares. 2. The trainer-facilitator tells the participants to label each square with one of the following terms: "Objects," "Attributes," "Relationships," and "Environment." 3. The trainer-facilitator asks each participant to fill in the four squares, giving responses that are reflective of his or her own department, division, etc., of the organization, generating as many responses as possible. The participants are allowed 10 minutes to complete this task. 4. After the 10-minute time limit has expired, the trainer-facilitator randomly selects three participants to share their responses. A time limit of 5 minutes should be established. 5. The trainer-facilitator breaks the group into groups of four. The exercise is repeated, with the trainer-facilitator restating steps 2 and 3. The participants are allowed 15 minutes to complete the task. 6. After the 15-minute time limit has expired, the trainer-facilitator asks the following question: "How can an organization engage in team building based on the various elements of its system?" Each group is asked to post a consensus response to this question on the newsprint. A time limit of 10 minutes should be established. 7. After the 10-minute time limit has expired, the trainer-facilitator asks each group to present its answer. After each group has presented, the trainer-facilitator opens up the floor for any comments and questions. A time limit of 10 minutes should be established.
Debriefing Questions:	• What characteristics do you share in common with other group members regarding the system elements? • What characteristics on the lists contribute to teamness? • What characteristics on the lists inhibit teamness? • What changes need to occur in order for us to work as a team in our organization?

Chapter Nine

How Does Our System Operate?

In the previous essay, the four elements of a system—objects, attributes, relationships, and interaction within the environment—were defined and explored. Now we need to turn our attention to how a system operates. Regardless of the type of organization that you belong to, every system follows four principles that guide the system into functioning properly. By examining these four principles, you will get a better idea of how your organization operates as a system.

In a sense, the process of baking a cake is similar to the process that an organization undergoes when operating as a system. These four principles include:

• *A cake is not just a cake.* When you examine a cake after it has come out of the oven, you notice the finished product, which is a result of combining all the necessary ingredients. Obviously, the cake is more than eggs, flour, and sugar. It is the combination of these three ingredients that makes the cake the way it appears. This is the same thing that occurs within our workplace. The principle of *nonsummativity* states that "the whole is greater than the sum of its parts." Our organization is composed of more than its separate departments. Rather, our organization is a combination of all of these departments *and* the people who work together to fulfill a specific function that the department requires. Each part can exist on its own, but each part must also come together with other parts to form a unified whole. Teams, too, follow the same principle. Like a cake, the end result is what is seen by others, but it has taken a required combination of ingredients in order to produce the result.

• *Leaving out an egg can cause the cake to fall.* If a recipe calls for three eggs and you leave out one egg, the cake will not rise as high as it could have. Why? Because the ingredients are interdependent—just like the parts of an organization. The principle of *interdependence* states that the function of one part affects the functions of other parts. Ultimately, this affects the output of the entire workplace. But what could cause a change in the function of one part? Actually, it could be anything, from a technological advancement to an interpersonal disagreement between two co-workers.

Change can affect the output of a department. Whenever this happens, the output of the entire workplace will be affected. While this does not mean that change or conflict will occur or will even be beneficial, the suggestion is that any irregularity can, and will, affect the entire organization. A team operates in the same way. Without cooperation of its members, a team will fall apart. Like a cake, the smooth functioning of our organization depends on all of its parts working together. If there is trouble with one part of the organization, it will be felt throughout the entire organization.

• *A cake will bake itself.* During the baking process, the ingredients in a cake mold together and combine to produce the finished product. In a sense, the cake regulates itself—no one is required to help the cake bake. This is true of our workplace too—only our ingredients are you, the employees. The principle of *self-regulation* states that the system has a process of regulating the behaviors and actions of its parts. We know that every organization has written, formal policies of some sort that regulate behaviors and actions, and that there are sanctions that would apply if the policies are broken. But we also know that our own organization has some "unwritten" codes or rules that regulate our behaviors and actions, and sanctions can be applied here as well.

Whether the policies are written or unwritten, some behaviors are tolerated and others are not, meaning that our organization will regulate the behaviors that are appropriate for the good of the organization. Whatever behaviors and actions are allowed depend on the organization, but the regulation depends on the organization as well. Like a cake, our organization will consider all the ingredients, and then combine and use them to the best potential ability. If an ingredient does not seem to blend well with the other ingredients or appears to affect the performance of the entire system, the organization must reconsider the use of the ingredient.

- *There is more than one way to bake a cake.* If you are going to bake a cake, you now have the option of baking it in either a microwave oven or a conventional oven. Perhaps you don't have the time to bake a cake, so you go to the local bakery and purchase one. In any case, you have a cake, and it does not matter how you got it. The principle of *equifinality* states that the end result can be achieved in many ways—the emphasis is not on the result, but on the various ways of achieving the result.

In terms of our organization, this means that we may have a goal in mind, and we have the option of selecting the way to achieve this goal. This is where the other principles of system operation come into play—our reliance on *you* is a necessary step to obtaining the best possible results for our organization.

Whether you are making a cake or working in your organization, the four principles that guide the operation of a system are similar. These principles can also be applied to the smooth functioning of a team. To become effective team members, you must stop and consider how these four principles affect your workplace and your team.

See the Chapter Thirty ABC Shoe Factory study for examples of how these principles occur in real organizations.

WORKOUT: WORK AT WORK

Purpose:	To illustrate the principles that guide system operation.
Group Size:	Any number up to 15 (Note: 1 role per person). Others may observe.
Time Required:	30 to 40 minutes.
Materials:	Role-playing cards (see Appendix A), group roles (see Appendix B), flipchart, paper, pencils.
Seating Arrangements:	No preference.
Other Considerations:	List of the 15 roles needs to be prepared ahead of time on the flipchart (see Appendix B).
Process:	1. The trainer-facilitator gives each participant a role-playing card that describes the role(s) that each participant will be playing. The trainer-facilitator reminds the participants to follow the directions on the notecard. The trainer-facilitator gives the participants five minutes to read and examine the notecards. 2. The trainer-facilitator announces that the group, as a whole, needs to develop a program to reduce absenteeism at work. The group is given 20 minutes to complete this task.
Debriefing Questions:	• What behaviors did you notice in others? • Which behaviors are necessary for the operation of a team? Which behaviors are not necessary? • Which behaviors might be sanctioned by other team members? • How did each group develop a solution? • How was the principle of *nonsummativity* demonstrated in this exercise? • How was the principle of *interdependence* realized in this exercise? • Which roles facilitated the *self-regulation* of the group? Which roles inhibited it? • How was the principle of *equifinality* demonstrated in this exercise? • How might the principles illustrated in this workout apply to a natural work group? How might the principles apply to where you are currently working?

Chapter Ten

We're All in This Together

"We're all in this together!" How many times have you heard that phrase at work? If everyone is in *this* together, then you need to communicate effectively with others in your workplace. *This* is the basis for teamwork! Communication is essential within departments and work teams. Communication between departments, between management and workers, and between supervisors and subordinates should be frequent, open, and trustworthy. If you can't communicate with the members of your team, how can anyone ever get anything accomplished?

The lack of effective communication affects several pieces in the organization puzzle: the individual employee, the departments or teams, and the organization as a whole. The individual must have a clear understanding of his/her role or his/her piece's fit in the puzzle in order to communicate with the other individuals and work as the team. Also, the department and teams need to have a clear understanding of their roles and fit with management and within the organization as a whole.

To help ensure this notion of quality communication between each of these key pieces of the organizational puzzle, researchers developed five work-setting characteristics. These dimensions should be considered an integral part of any development within the organizational puzzle. The five key elements of managing work settings or organization puzzles are as follows:

1. Managing work efficiently in a changing and complex environment. To get quality output, you must adapt to changing activities in the workplace. Each puzzle piece has a designated place within the puzzle, and when the puzzle changes, the pieces must shift and move to adapt to the change. Effectively communicating the need and reason for the change is crucial.

2. Communicating with others in the team and seeking feedback. The puzzle pieces must keep constant lines of communication open with those pieces around them as well as seeking feedback and responses from surrounding pieces.

3. Standardizing the work roles and procedures. This allows members to know what is expected and promotes continuity and stability in work activities. When the puzzle board is clearly designed, the pieces know where they fit and what their expected roles and responsibilities are within the puzzle.

4. Standardizing response and performance of job tasks. This requirement, performing tasks as demanded, ensures that as the parts of the whole are completed, eventually the whole will be completed. By forming the procedure and sequence in which to fit the pieces into place, efficient and effective work settings or puzzles are formed.

5. Managing for effectiveness when dealing with external forces. Members of an organization need to be aware of the external forces such as the stock market, changing technology, laws, and competition, which all have an effect on decisions. External forces can also be categorized as crisis management situations. Unlike planned change, external forces can disturb or improve the organization puzzle. Management and other pieces need to effectively react to such forces.

Each of these key elements should be remembered in order to maintain quality communication between management and teams and help ensure a successful fit in the organizational puzzle.

See the Chapter Thirty One Harwood Pajama Factory study for examples of role relationship expectations in the workplace.

WORKOUT: PIECING IT TOGETHER

Purpose: To create an awareness of quality communication and effective productivity.

Group Size: Nine participants. Others may observe.

Time Required: 10 to 15 minutes.

Materials: Scissors, puzzle gameboard, puzzle pieces (see Appendix C).

Seating Arrangement: At a table where all participants are able to be at one end to view the activity gameboard from the same angle.

Other Considerations: None.

Process:
1. Each person takes an identical puzzle piece. (Note: Each piece should be numbered 1 through 9.) The puzzle piece number determines where the person is located on the game board.
2. The gameboard is set up and explained by the trainer-facilitator. The trainer-facilitator makes the following statement: "Each of you is a puzzle piece of the company. Picture your puzzle piece as a department within the company and the outer border as management. As you can see, managers, located on the edge of the gameboard, already have the shape of their puzzle piece tabs established. Your job is to cut out, in an appropriate shape, the tabs of your puzzle piece to fit into management and the other pieces around you. Using effective communication, your goal is to be able to successfully fit your puzzle piece into the company puzzle to complete the organization's product. You have to negotiate with those around you as to the shape of the tab or cut into your piece. Plan before you cut!"

Debriefing Questions:
- How did you feel when you had to communicate about the shape of the tab with the others around you?
- Did you dislike cutting your puzzle piece away? Would you rather have the adjoining tab be cut away instead?
- How did the puzzle piece holders adapt to changes and complexity of puzzle piece tab decisions?
- How was feedback shared among group members in making decisions to cut up pieces?
- How were role expectations achieved? How did you know what was expected of you by others? How was this task accomplished?
- How did the group complete the puzzle? What tasks were performed to facilitate or inhibit the group?
- Were there any external forces that affected the group's solution to the puzzle?
- What is the relationship between the give-and-take in a workplace such as your own? What have you had to "cut away" and negotiate in your workplace?
- What other kinds of interactions occurred during the activity? What other discussions occurred?

Chapter Eleven And Now for the Weather…

Take a moment and think about the communication in your workplace. Imagine that you are tossing out ideas about a project that you have just been assigned. How do your co-workers react to your ideas? Perhaps they greet your ideas with a chilly reception, and their comments are as cold as ice. On the other hand, perhaps your ideas result in sparkles of enthusiasm radiating from your colleagues. Maybe you receive a shower of compliments, or maybe you feel as if someone has rained on your parade.

The responses you receive from your colleagues are what we are referring to as the communication climate of your workplace. Typically, the communication climate is regarded as being either supportive or defensive. A supportive climate means that communication among workers is valued and encouraged. On the other hand, a defensive communication climate means that speakers risk being shot down. At work, we are the recipient of remarks and comments that represent the emotional tone of our interpersonal relationships. Like the weather, the communication climate will have an effect on how we feel at any given point during any given day.

Fortunately, we have all been in situations where we feel our communication is welcomed by our co-workers, and we feel our contributions are valued. On the other hand, we have also been in a situation where we feel as if our communication has been restricted, and our comments were not considered as being important or meaningful.

A work team especially requires that a supportive communication climate be established. The communication climate is not a given—it is determined by the team members. Like the weather, the communication climate of a team can become unpredictable and can vary before leveling off. Before you put away your rainwear, you need to be aware of some techniques that will help you and your team members develop and maintain a sunny climate.

As a team member, you can help establish a sunny climate by acting as a weatherperson. The tips for forecasting a supportive climate include:

• *Be descriptive rather than evaluative.* It is often too easy for us to evaluate another person or an idea rather than describe our reactions to another person or idea. An evaluative statement is usually judgmental and has a "you" direction—for example, one might say "Your idea doesn't make any sense. Obviously *you* didn't think before you spoke." A descriptive statement, rather, has an "I" orientation, and does not blame or fault the other individual. In this case, one could say, "I hear what you are saying, but *I'm* not understanding the idea. Could you explain the third step again?" Describing, instead of evaluating, promotes a supportive climate and will encourage your team members to express themselves.

• *Be empathic rather than neutral.* Remember the saying "don't judge a man until you have walked in his shoes"? This statement is a good example of empathy. If you are empathic, it means that you accept another person's feelings without feeling sorry for that person. At times, though, we feel neutral, and we think that this feeling is acceptable. But neutrality suggests indifference toward the speaker or the topic. Being neutral also suggests that you don't have a positive attitude toward another person. Rather than act neutral, act empathic! Using empathy helps the team effort by focusing on the message, and not the individual. For example, suppose you are typing a report on your computer and somehow it gets erased on the hard drive. When you tell a teammate, the teammate could say "Oh well—it happens" (a *neutral* response) or could say "Gee, that is too bad. I know exactly how you feel" (an *empathic* response). Being empathic instead of being neutral will help you and your team develop trust and feelings of camaraderie.

- *Treat each other as equals and not superiors.* Treating each other with equality means that you see and accept each other for what you are, and not for what you could be or what you want someone to be. At times, we are judgmental and believe that there is only one way to behave and think—which is usually *our* way. When we behave in this manner, we are acting superior. Unfortunately, this is not effective. In an earlier essay, we stated that a system is composed of objects and their attributes. What we also need to mention is that you need to accept each object and its attributes regardless of your feelings toward that object. As a team member, you will probably engage in participatory decision making, and it is essential that mutual trust and respect be present. Acting in a superior manner communicates that you don't want to relate or exist on equal terms with your teammates. Using equality instead of superiority allows your team to become cohesive and bond as one.

By using these strategies, you should be able to establish and promote a supportive communication climate within your team. This is not to say that communication will always be bright, positive, and sunny. Occasionally, your team will have a gloomy day. But with some effort and work, the outlook will always include good weather.

See in Chapter Thirty One The Aircraft Studies for understanding the importance of a supportive climate.

Chapter 11 / And Now for the Weather...

WORKOUT: RAIN, RAIN, GO AWAY!

Purpose: To illustrate the concept of supportive climate.

Group Size: Any number.

Time Required: 20 to 30 minutes.

Materials: Gamepiece (for example, use a beanbag. Make one side yellow; make one side black), award ribbons.

Seating Arrangements: In a circle.

Other Considerations: None.

Process:
1. The trainer-facilitator explains the following ground rules: (a) the gamepiece will be tossed from one participant to another; (b) the gamepiece can be tossed to any participant in any order; and (c) when each participant receives the gamepiece, he or she should make a comment about the group that is reflective of the color on the gamepiece.
2. The trainer-facilitator reads the following paragraph to the participants: "This gamepiece has two sides: one side has a bright color, and the other side has a dark color. Each color represents the type of statement that you will address to the group. If the gamepiece lands on the side with the bright color, you make a supportive remark about the group. If the gamepiece lands on the side with the dark color, you must make a negative statement about the group and then make a positive statement about the group. After you make your statement, you throw the gamepiece to another participant but only after the group, through consensus, has agreed that your comment reflects a supportive climate."
3. The process continues until everyone has had a chance to participate.
4. After the conclusion, the trainer-facilitator presents each participant with an award ribbon.

Debriefing Questions:
- What characteristics reflected a supportive communication climate? Give examples of those statements that were:

  Descriptive statements about the group.
  Empathic statements creating trust or demonstrating feelings of camaraderie.
  Equality statements that demonstrated commonality of group "we"-ness.

- What characteristics reflected a defensive communication climate? Give examples of those statements that were:

  Evaluative statements that judged group members or performance.
  Neutral statements that indicated self-centered communication "I" statements, not "we" statements.
  Superiority statements that gave the impression to the group that certain individuals were superior or better than the group.

Chapter Twelve # Uncommon Sense

In colonial days, New England settlers built their dwellings clustered on the perimeter of land they had cleared in which each family pastured sheep and cows. That clearing came to be called "the commons." As settlements grew into villages, and communities and towns became cities, their residents no longer shared a common pasture. Yet, the concept of "the commons" has lived on in New England and refers to a green place for community gatherings.

In colonial days, an individual's personal, work, and community life were inextricably connected. Everyone in a small town knew the butcher, the baker, the candlestick maker, and their families. The welfare of one was entwined with the well-being of all.

The industrial revolution and the population explosion changed that common interdependence. Today, where we work is often distant from where we live. More often than not, our places of work are headquartered in another state or abroad, owned by people with whom we will never communicate.

The rest of the story is that we exploited the environment. Just as some of the settlers greedily raised more and more livestock on the commons causing them to be overgrazed, we plowed and overfarmed the land, eroding the soil. Two centuries later, the story hasn't changed.

We are facing these powerful forces that can destroy us—the survival of the fittest, which unleashes the greed of taking advantage of the less able and the exploitation of the environment that uncontrolled competition leaves in its wake. The biologist Garrett Hardin calls this the "tragedy of the commons." Our one hope for creating a sustainable environment—one in which we do not overfish the seas and do not mess up the land we farm and air we breathe—is that we must make the hard decisions and do the hard work so that the commons remain available.

WORKOUT: DOMINOS AND INTERDEPENDENCE

Purpose: To demonstrate team interdependence.

Group Size: Clusters of five to eight participants.

Time Required: 20 to 30 minutes.

Materials: A box of dominos, markers, and newsprint for each table of five to eight participants.

Seating Arrangement: Tables seating five to eight participants.

Other Considerations: None.

Process:
1. Each table is given five minutes to set up a domino-effect configuration that represents connections and interdependence within a workplace.
2. At the end of the time limit, each table is given five minutes to explain its configuration to the larger group, and then to demonstrate a potential event or act that could create a domino effect. A variation is for a group to set up a configuration that demonstrates how the workplace is so structured that a domino effect would not be experienced.

Debriefing Questions: Each group should be allowed 10 minutes to post its answers (on newsprint) to the following questions.

- In what ways should a workplace be organized to benefit from a domino effect? In what ways should a workplace be organized so that a domino effect does not damage other work groups?
- How did your table determine what configuration it would build to illustrate the domino effect?
- What might you do as an individual to improve your interdependent relationships with co-workers? What might your work group do to improve its working connection with other work units?

Chapter 12/Uncommon Sense

WORKOUT: GET ALL YOU CAN

Purpose: To illustrate how people can make agreements that work for the best interest of the group.

Group Size: Five participants. Others (up to 30) may observe.

Time Required: 10 to 20 minutes.

Materials: A supply of small objects (paper clips, rubber bands, steel nuts, candy kisses, bubble gum, pennies, etc.).

Seating Arrangements: Five chairs around a small table.

Other Considerations: After the first group of five participants completes the activity, the activity may be repeated by having each player select an observer to take her or his place at the table.

Process:
1. The trainer-facilitator places 10 of the small objects in the center of the table.
2. The trainer-facilitator announces "start" and "stop" in 5-second intervals. At the announcement of each "start," each participant may take as many objects as she or he desires. The trainer-facilitator informs the participants that talking is not allowed.
3. Objects left on the common playing surface after each 5 second round will be duplicated in kind (for example, two paper clips that remain will have two more paper clips added to the pile).
4. The game ends when there are no more objects on the table; however, the trainer-facilitator can stop the game at any point. The following questions can be asked to the group.

Debriefing Questions:
- What happened? Who took what? What caused the game to end?
- How do you feel about your behavior and the behavior of the other participants?
- How does this exercise reflect life? For example, what does the rule represent that says *the leader can stop the game whenever she or he chooses?*
- What does the game illustrate? What does the table represent (in light of the previous essay)? Why is *harvesting* an appropriate word when taking objects from the table?
- What does this game illustrate about yourself and the other players?
- What might your workplace do to protect the interests that it holds in common with other organizations?
- Does rewarding individual effort benefit your place of work?

MOTIVATION

Chapter 13   Teamwork
Chapter 14   Head over Heels
Chapter 15   It Begins with Me
Chapter 16   Presentations Made Easy

Chapter Thirteen
Teamwork

It is interesting how the metaphor of teamwork is so effective in communicating to people the maximization of each individual's talents in a climate of mutual respect. A team player's aim is to develop a sense of unity. This sense of unity, in turn, maximizes the accomplishment of a shared goal.

In the workplace, a team is most often considered as any group that shares the same superior or follows the same orders. What distinguishes a group from a team, however, is that a team has spirit. With this spirit, the team can meet any particular pressing goal the organization might require. Once a group becomes a team, we have it made. The question is how to develop the spirit of teamwork within a group.

One idea is to develop what is called a "temporary society," in which people come together from diverse areas within an organization to share ideas and solve problems. For example, Japanese organizations practice job rotation, where employees change their jobs and work in different units every few months, so that they get a sense of how the organization functions as a whole.

But not everyone in an organization is aware that the units combine to function as a whole. If employees are informed how their units are integrated into the system as a whole, they will respond more quickly in times of need.

The idea that organizations should compete against each other and thereby maximize their performance in a spirit of competition is not gone. We are now living in a fast paced world with technology that speeds up information retrieval. This new information makes it necessary for an organization to be able to mobilize quickly, and in response to the new realities that new information can create.

In order for different functional areas to be able to adapt to change, management systems must be developed carefully. Management systems refer to communication, decision making, control systems, and leadership. Organizational processes such as a board of directors, which unify operations and people, should also be examined. It is important to give attention to the team building climate that is created within the organization's structure and system. The spirit of any organization is critical to its success.

Chris Argyris, an expert on organizational behavior, suggests that teams follow 10 rules to generate a supportive team-building climate:

1. Contributions made within the group are additive.
2. The group moves forward as a unit with a strong sense of team spirit.
3. Decisions are made by consensus.
4. Strong commitment to decisions is made by group members.
5. The group continually evaluates itself.
6. The group is clear about its goals.
7. Conflict is handled in an open manner.
8. Alternative solutions are generated.
9. Leadership should go to the individual most qualified to lead the team at that particular point.
10. Feelings are handled in an open manner.

These ideas can serve as standards by which any group can test and review its own working relationship. For additional information, refer to Chapter Two and the section in Chapter Thirty Three on National Training Laboratories: T-Groups.

WORKOUT: BRAINSTORMING

Purpose:	To increase employee involvement in the task of problem-solving solutions.
Group Size:	Any number.
Time Required:	20 to 30 minutes.
Materials:	Newsprint pads, markers, paper, pens.
Seating Arrangement:	In small clusters spread around the room with newsprint and markers located near each cluster.
Other Considerations:	None.

Process:

1. The trainer-facilitator chooses a specific task for the group beforehand. For example, the group could develop a system for your company to reward employees.
2. The trainer-facilitator introduces the topic of brainstorming: "Brainstorming can be described as a step in problem solving and/or a method for obtaining a maximum number of ideas for group consideration. The only rule is to toss out as many ideas as possible without criticism by anyone."
3. The trainer-facilitator divides the seminar participant group into teams of two, three, and six. Each team must select one participant to act as the secretary and list all the ideas generated.
4. The trainer-facilitator instructs the teams to list on newsprint as many ways as they can that might be useful, for example, in rewarding employees for good work. The teams are given 10 minutes to accomplish this task.
5. Each team posts its list of ideas on the newsprint pad.

Debriefing Questions:

- Did everyone get a chance to put in his or her ideas?
- Were you able to avoid criticizing others' contributions?
- Did the group arrive at any good ideas? bad ideas?
- What did you think of this as a method of problem solving?
- What are the advantages of brainstorming in a group?
- What are the disadvantages of brainstorming in a group?
- How can we prevent individuals from squelching good ideas?
- Brainstorming is the first step in a problem-solving process. What other steps does the group need to take before further problem solving can occur?

Chapter Fourteen   # Head over Heels

Like the argument about the glass of water being half empty or half full, the word "motivation" and its cousin "enthusiasm" probably get more *love or hate* reaction than any other words heard in the workplace. Those who love hearing these words already see themselves as highly motivated and enthusiastic, and they can't get enough—motivational tapes, books, or affirmations, all with the message, like Muhammad Ali, that "I'm the greatest!"

But those who don't share this positive reaction are seen as being negative, too slow, no fun, and holding everyone else back. They, in turn, view the motivation buffs as wild-eyed chest pounders who fill themselves with a lot of hype and who try to push their gospel onto everyone else. It seems we are either wildly for or against the concepts of motivation and enthusiasm. Hardly anyone is indifferent.

If one is indifferent, it may be that the ideas that guide motivation and enthusiasm are not clear. Instead of presenting a clear message, the proponent pushes the gospel harder. Enthusiasm in general means nothing. If there is one truth even a hardheaded realist will buy, it is the fact that *you can't get motivated or enthusiastic over nothing.* Realizing this idea can open a lot of doors.

Even the biggest pessimist is an optimist in planning a vacation. A totally pessimistic vacation planner doesn't exist because the person never goes anywhere. Why plan something that will fail? Each summer millions of Americans are on the roads and in the airports going somewhere and expecting to have a good time—and they are all motivated and enthused.

What's the secret? Simply, the vacation was planned. A goal was set and work was done on that goal to ensure a favorable outcome. If we can't get motivated or enthusiastic over nothing, we certainly can get motivated or enthusiastic over something. If millions of people have fun on vacations, those same millions also had just as much fun planning for and anticipating the vacation.

If both optimists and pessimists get excited over their vacation goals, could they also get excited over achieving goals at work? Admittedly, work might not be as much fun as a vacation. But we've all experienced those great days at work: the big project is finally completed, the millionth piece came off its line, the deadline is met. Some of these accomplishments are cause for companywide or departmentwide celebrations.

Motivation and enthusiasm need not always involve a huge goal. Personally, we sometimes have had great days when our project was completed, production or quality was the highest ever for our shift, the most sales were made, or a problem was solved. If we can personally plan to reach these goals, goal attainment is that much sweeter.

What would happen to motivation in the workplace if clear-cut goals were set, if everyone had a chance to give input in the planning of those goals, and if everyone felt a part of the achievement of those goals? Co-workers would feel motivated and enthusiastic because something real was accomplished and because each individual helped make it happen.

WORKOUT: GO(AL) AHEAD!

Purpose: To illustrate goal setting.

Group Size: 6 to 40 participants.

Time Required: 20 to 30 minutes.

Materials: Toy building blocks.

Seating Arrangements: In groups at separate tables.

Other Considerations: None.

Process:
1. The trainer-facilitator assigns participants into equal size groups of four to six people.
2. The trainer-facilitator informs the groups that they have 10 minutes to build the "best" building with the blocks provided. No further directions will be provided.
3. At the end of the 10 minutes, the trainer-facilitator may lead a discussion using the following questions.

Debriefing Questions:
- Did your group have any problems?
- Was your group frustrated at any point?
- What was your group's goal during this exercise?
- How did your group achieve its goal? How important is a goal to a work group?
- Did you negotiate with other groups to achieve your goal? If so, why? If not, why not?
- Did your group work as a team? If so, how? If not, why not?
- How did members contribute to goal achievement?
- After the debriefing, jot down several ways this exercise could be applied to job-related goals.

_____

_____

_____

_____

Chapter Fifteen

It Begins with Me

A sales manager was asked about her main problem with her employees. Immediately she answered, "lack of enthusiasm and motivation." Why is lack of enthusiasm and motivation an attitude problem in the workplace? Because enthusiasm sells. That's right, enthusiasm sells!

Enthusiasm, motivation, and involvement are all elements that contribute to innovation within businesses. If employees feel that their input is considered and that they are involved in planning goals, they are more likely to relax and contribute. Conversely, when contributions to their jobs are rewarded, employees become more motivated and involved. What is the result of this involvement? Usually increased profits. Profits increase because employees fix problems they would otherwise have ignored. Employees are more interested in customer satisfaction and quality control when they take pride in and identify positively with their workplace. Enthusiastic employees extend their enthusiasm to the products of the company. This same principle also applies to government agencies and nonprofit organizations.

Enthusiastic employees also spread their enthusiasm to other employees within the team. Imagine the difference between being greeted with a sincere "good morning" as opposed to a grunt. A bad attitude affects other employees' morale. A negative tone can penetrate the entire staff and rain on anyone's parade. Some people may think that it's sophisticated while others may think that it's "cool" not to show emotion or enthusiasm. Many people believe that enthusiasm is for naive, childlike people. But ask yourself this question—are people really happier being alienated from other people? There are those who drudge through the day waiting for it to end. Life is boring and unfulfilling for cynical people.

At least part of what makes a dull job duller is an employee's life-is-the-pits attitude. An attitude is powerful, and we propose to you that it would be to your benefit to work on employee enthusiasm. Children are naturally enthusiastic. It is only when they learn to become cynical that they grow up to be inhibited. Enthusiasm not only improves a person's personality, but it also makes people like that person more.

Some employers argue that enthusiasm is not one of their personality traits. Traits are not given at birth and personalities do change—some become sour, some become cheerleaders. But teams play and work because of cheerleaders. It is cheerleader enthusiasm, not words, that is powerful. In hundreds of small ways, you can be the spark that brightens the workday. Enthusiasm allows you to reach out to others—you can make them aware that they need to laugh a bit and can convey to them that you are someone who will laugh with them.

You probably want to know where to begin. The first place to begin is by talking to yourself. If you empty your mind of unhappy thoughts, just as you empty your pockets every night before going to bed, you won't be carrying around your worries the next day. If you decide first thing in the morning to be enthusiastic, then it will be more possible to think positive thoughts.

It is best to begin with a mental process of seeing yourself as a completely positive person. If people act as if they have enthusiasm, they eventually will have it! You must take charge of your thoughts instead of allowing your thoughts to control you. Enthusiasm should be made a top priority in your life!

Employees and their managers should be encouraged to hang in there, stick with it, and hammer it out until a feeling of enthusiasm takes over. The key is to visualize, energize, and actualize.

Finally, to be a successful team, co-workers have to give their all. Giving your all is not simply getting your feet wet. If these suggestions are followed, we assure you that you will become more enthusiastic, and this enthusiasm will surface in the faces of those in your work group and those with whom the work group is connected.

Chapter 15/It Begins with Me

WORKOUT: JUST FOR TODAY

Purpose: To improve enthusiasm.

Group Size: Any number.

Time Required: 20 minutes.

Materials: None.

Seating Arrangement: No preference.

Other Considerations: None.

Process:

1. The trainer-facilitator instructs the participants to think about how they could specifically be more enthusiastic in their daily work activities and to write these ideas down in the space below. The group is given 5 minutes to complete this task.

- Ways to improve enthusiasm during daily work activities.

_____
_____
_____
_____
_____

2. When the task is completed, the trainer-facilitator instructs the participants to think of arousing words (such as "dynamic" or "fantastic") that imply enthusiasm and to list these words in the space below. The group is given five minutes to complete this task.

- Words that imply enthusiasm.

_____
_____
_____
_____
_____

3. The trainer-facilitator instructs the participants to use the lists as a reference for their daily activities. The trainer-facilitator tells the participants to refer to these two lists whenever a problem arises during the workday.

Debriefing Questions:

- As a group, what words imply enthusiasm?
- How can the enthusiasm that accompanies leisure activity be incorporated into the workplace?
- In what way has this exercise been useful in defining enthusiasm?

Chapter Sixteen

Presentations Made Easy

"Congratulations! Your team has just been invited to present a proposal to improve a work process to management." Most of us would greet this announcement with mixed emotions. If we're on a team, we are expected to participate. If the team is going to "talk shop," we're going to have to say something. And if we have to say something on behalf of the team, that sounds suspiciously like a speech!

But giving a team report does not mean you have to panic. Instead, working with others on a presentation can provide benefits that would not be possible working alone.

One benefit of working as a team is that the number of ideas and suggestions, as well as the amount of information, increases. Developing alternatives and solutions to problems can be more thoroughly examined and evaluated when a team works together. Remember—the preparation of a presentation is as important as the delivery. In this case, again, none of us is as smart as all of us!

Another benefit is that we learn how to interact with others in our quest to develop a presentational style unique to our team. If one person enjoys introductions, let that person plan the opening. If another team member is good at clarifying and summarizing main points, let that member develop the transitions. The important thing is that we should be ourselves. We should be honored to be chosen as being part of the team. The ways in which we communicate individually contribute to the ways in which the team communicates.

The third benefit is that not all team members have to speak. Some people simply enjoy the experience of public speaking, whereas others shy away from the task. But even the more timid individuals on your team may surprise everyone by adding some bits of information the more talkative members have failed to mention.

Haven't we all, at one time or another, listened to a speaker who impressed us with his or her speaking ability? We might admire that person and even secretly wish we could speak the same way. By working together as a team, we can learn about the speaking process and even develop tips that can make each of us a better speaker.

One of the more helpful tips for a team presentation is handmade visual aids—the kind of diagrams and problem-solving charts your team has made during the course of researching a problem. So the next time your work group is asked to make a presentation, think about the advantages of working together as a team.

WORKOUT: READY, SET, GO!

Purpose: To demonstrate key principles of team presentations.

Group Size: Any number of groups of five.

Time Required: 30 to 90 minutes.

Materials: None.

Seating Arrangement: Each group should be seated at a table some distance from the other groups.

Other Considerations: This activity is most appropriate after groups have arrived at a proposal that they want or need to present.

Process:

1. The trainer-facilitator announces that the group will work together as a team.
2. The trainer-facilitator instructs the team to give a short informational speech on the topic of a workplace improvement.
3. Each group should complete the three steps of effective team presentations.
4. After each group has completed its preparation, the trainer-facilitator instructs each team to present its report to the larger group. Reports should be restricted to 10 minutes.
5. At the conclusion of each report, other participants should direct questions to the group. Questions should be restricted to the content presented in the group's report. Members of the presenting group should take turns answering the questions. The question-answer period should be limited to 10 minutes.

The Three Steps of Effective Team Presentations:

- Step 1: What ideas and suggestions does the group want presented?

  _____
  _____
  _____
  _____

- Step 2: Who will be responsible for preparing parts of the presentation?

Team Member	Responsibility

- Step 3: Who will be responsible for delivering the:

Team Member	Duty
_____	Introduction
_____	Presenting the Problem
_____	Presenting Causes
_____	Presenting Solutions
_____	Handling Questions

Debriefing Questions:
- What aspects of the reports would you rate as impressive? What aspects could use some improvement?
- Was the question-answer period effective?
- How did members of your group show support for those who were speaking?

LISTENING

Chapter 17 Listening Is a Team Effort
Chapter 18 When the Ball Is in Your Court
Chapter 19 Improving Your Team's Listening Skills

Chapter Seventeen

Listening Is a Team Effort

Who taught you how to listen? Chances are the only instructions you ever received in listening came from your parents and teachers. "Keep quiet!" "Pay attention!" "Listen," they told you. But did they tell you what listening is? Or that different situations require a different style of listening? Probably not!

Listening is the conscious effort we must make if we want to make sense of the noise we hear around us. In the business world, listening is hard work. Noises fill the environment, such as machinery, telephones, and radio. But people make noises, too! Customers, clients, co-workers, bosses, and employees all come to us for different reasons. Therefore, each encounter requires a different type of listening. For example, listening to a friend recount "the big game" is not the same as trying to take an order, solve a problem, or evaluate a sales pitch.

Unfortunately, our parents and teachers never told us that there is more than one way to listen. They assumed that if you kept quiet and paid attention, listening came naturally. Listening actively, empathically, nonjudgmentally, and critically are key skills for team players. Each requires a different way of thinking as we listen. By examining the four styles of listening, you will be able to get an idea on how to listen.

Listen actively. As the name implies, this type of listening requires that you take an active role in the situation at hand. You may need to ask questions, pose hypothetical situations, probe for more information, seek clarification, or restate a message to check your perceptions of what the speaker has said.

Active listening is useful in decision-making tasks, when receiving instructions, when trying to solve problems, and when gathering data. It is the kind of listening we might use when trying to analyze the wants and needs of our employees, our customers, or our organization. Keep in mind that active listening can also be empathic, nonjudgmental, and critical.

Listen empathically. Empathic listening is based on understanding the other person. Empathic listening does not require that you agree with her or him. It simply means that you are willing to take the time and view a situation from a perspective other than your own.

Empathic listening can increase your own awareness and understanding of a problem. It can be the first step toward breaking a serious deadlock in negotiations or helping two parties identify a common ground.

Listen nonjudgmentally. Being nonjudgmental means that you are willing to keep an open mind. This includes suspending judgment and reserving opinions.

Unfortunately, many of us do not listen to someone because we do not want to hear what the person has to say or we assume that we already know what will be said because we are already familiar with the problem. Listening objectively and suspending judgments long enough to give customers or employees a chance to be heard can defuse an otherwise volatile situation. More important, by listening nonjudgmentally to all sides of an issue, we may be able to get to the "real" root of a problem.*

Listen critically. Critical listening is used when an evaluation or assessment has to be made and is, therefore, essential to problem solving and analyzing data.

When using critical listening, some type of standard is necessary for making comparisons and evaluations. These can vary from a formal list of specific behaviors to an informal series of questions to be answered. For example, are there flaws in the plan? Is the logic sound? Will the plan meet our needs?

Critical listeners do not waste time making snap judgments or negative comments. Instead, they carefully weigh the pros and cons of all decisions as they listen. They know that when they are uncertain, it is important to ask *what* and *why* questions. When critical listeners are asked to establish commitment to a project, they know it is important to ask *when, where,* and *what is expected* questions.

The key to being a good team player is to know *when* and *how* to listen effectively.

---

* Notice that styles #2 and #3 are the same suggestions made in Chapter Eleven.

WORKOUT: LISTEN AND YOU WILL HEAR

Purpose: To demonstrate the process of critical listening.

Group Size: Any number.

Time Required: 20 minutes.

Materials: Pencils, paper, script for trainer-facilitator (see Appendix D).

Seating Arrangement: No preference.

Other Considerations: Participants may not take notes.

Process:

1. The trainer-facilitator reads the script to the participants (see Appendix D: Test Your Critical Listening Skills). *Note: Participants should not look at Appendix D ahead of time.*

2. After the trainer-facilitator has read the script (Appendix D), each participant should answer the following questions:

- How much money does George make an hour?

- How many hours of work did George miss?

- How many hours did it take George to complete the job by himself?

- How much money did George save by doing the job himself?

3. After the test is completed, the trainer-facilitator reads the answers, and each participant checks his/her answer. Each participant completes the second set of questions (see below). The trainer-facilitator can then lead a debriefing.

- How many answers did you get correct?

- What role does listening play in the work group?

- What kind of relationship exists between the listener and the speaker?

- Which listening skills do you think you need to work on?

  _____

  _____

  _____

Debriefing Questions:
- What facilitated your listening and success in answering questions?
- What inhibited your ability to listen to the story and answer the questions accurately?
- How did you exhibit each of the following listening behaviors: active, empathic, nonjudgmental, and critical?
- What could you have done to become a more effective listener?
- How did the lack of feedback affect your ability to interpret the story?

Chapter Eighteen

When the Ball Is in Your Court

Learning how to listen competently and effectively lies in the listener's ability to respond appropriately to a message. But to give the proper type of feedback that acknowledges our understanding of the speaker's message is not always the easiest thing to do. Unfortunately, our understanding may not be quite as clear as it should be. Other times, situations arise that we are not prepared to handle at any given moment. But do we always acknowledge these facts? Not very often.

A variety of feedback devices can be used to improve our listening skills and improve our understanding of another person's purpose and meaning. Each device is important when working with team members. Because some devices work better in one situation than in another, we address each of them individually. These feedback devices include the following elements.

Advising. "You should...". This is one of the most popular and one of the least effective types of responses to use. It is an ego trip for the listener and can often be harmful to the sender.

However, in the workplace, it is often necessary. If advice must be given, two things must be known: Is it right? And is it wanted or welcomed by the person? Many good relationships have turned sour because of *too* much advice. If you have to give advice, it is best to suggest your ideas as tentative.

Judging. "That's great (awful)...". Judging is also one of the most popular, yet least helpful, listening responses. It, too, is an ego offering from the listener that often proves detrimental to a relationship.

But in the workplace, judgments are essential. It doesn't matter if you are the boss or one of a thousand employees—make sure your judgments are accurate and based on sound criteria, not ego or personal bias.

Analyzing. "Your problem seems to be...". In personal relationships, analyzing is another type of ego response. It is best used in problem-solving situations. Two rules to remember when using analysis: make sure analysis of the problem is based on hard data and make sure your analysis is welcomed.

Questioning. "What do you think...". This is one of the safest and wisest responses, provided you do not sound like an interrogator. However, it is quite useful if you are uncertain about the details of the situation or how to handle it.

You may choose to ask the person to repeat the remark, just in case you missed something important. This occurs quite frequently, and unless we check our perceptions, we cannot be sure both of us are on the same wavelength. Unfortunately, many people are afraid they may sound foolish or appear to be ignorant.

Supporting. "You'll be OK...". Supporting responses are often used to encourage a speaker to continue talking or to bolster the other person's sagging ego. Responses can vary from a few choice words to a friendly pat on the back. Such responses can also double as a form of acknowledgment, such as when a manager or supervisor encounters a subordinate at work. Rather than ignoring the worker, a friendly greeting or gesture in passing offered by the superior reinforces the team concept. In this respect, a team manager assumes the role of ego booster and coach.

Prompting. "I'm listening, go ahead...". This type of response is used to encourage the speaker to continue. It may solicit more information or simply serve as a supporting response. Like other responses, prompting can be nonverbal as well as verbal.

Responses of this type are invaluable to an employee when attempting to discuss a situation with another employee. These responses help ease tension the speaker may be experiencing, and they reassure the speaker you are interested in what he or she has to say.

Paraphrasing. "Let me get this straight, you seem to be saying ...". Paraphrasing is simply a restatement of a speaker's words in a different form. The purpose of paraphrasing is twofold. First, rephrasing a speaker's words can help clarify his/her own thoughts, particularly if the speaker has not identified the problem. Second, paraphrasing is used to check your perceptions and understanding of the other person's statement, such as "did you say that...".

It is the ego of the individual that most often blocks the path of a team effort. The fear of loss of power or appearing to be less than perfect creates many misunderstandings. Such problems and misunderstandings are not only detrimental to the team, but they can also be quite costly.

WORKOUT: BOUNCING MESSAGES

Purpose: To demonstrate the types of feedback processes.

Group Size: Any even number (participants will be placed in dyads).

Time Required: 10 to 20 minutes.

Materials: A handout with the list of the seven feedback devices (one copy for each participant).

Seating Arrangement: No preference.

Other Considerations: Activity works best if the participants are not acquainted with one another beforehand.

Process:
1. The trainer-facilitator places participants in dyads by asking the participants to select a partner whom they do not already know.
2. The participants are instructed to talk with one another about their relationships with their co-workers. Observers can record the seven types of feedback devices used. After 10 minutes, the group returns to its original seating arrangement.

Debriefing Questions:
- Which feedback devices were most frequently used? Why?
- Which feedback devices were least frequently used? Why?
- Which feedback devices were the most helpful? the least helpful?
- How can feedback devices be used effectively in a work group?
- Role play an effective use of each of the following feedback devices: paraphrasing, supporting, prompting, and questioning.

Chapter Nineteen

Improving Your Team's Listening Skills

Effective listening is the backbone of any team effort. It determines whether the communication climate within that team will be supportive or defensive. Shared leadership implies that all team members have a responsibility for making the team effort work. If one team member fails to listen carefully, the whole team suffers.

Learning to listen takes time, care, and practice. Suddenly changing your behaviors can create distrust in a working relationship. However, developing good listening skills can become a group goal in which each member works to support one another's progress. These skills include:

Develop an open mind. Consider the advantages of knowing many things about many topics. In conversation, a broad knowledge of several topics can help you feel more comfortable and make you a more interesting person to be around. One method of keeping an open mind is to ask questions that reflect your interest about a subject.

Find the proper setting. Try to choose a place for your conversations as free from physical and psychological distractions as possible. Choose a place to have a serious discussion that will allow full concentration from you, your partner, and your teammates.

Examine yourself for biases. Be aware of your biases and guard against letting them prejudice the message. Although you may have held a certain opinion for a long time, each new speaker deserves the chance to tell you what he or she knows about a topic. New insights may be available to you, and you may discover someone whose company and support you appreciate.

Take notes. Do not be afraid to take notes. Notes can help you focus on the main points of the message. Later, referring to your notes will help you organize the message so you can remember it more accurately and evaluate it more objectively. As you list points in your notes, ask yourself about them. Consider how well the ideas fit together and how well the evidence supports the points as compared to what you already know.

Reserve judgment. Do not interrupt the speaker! Do not make up your mind until you have heard the entire message. Although you may think you know the direction in which the speaker is headed, he or she may introduce new information at the end of the message that will require you to reconsider your position. By reserving judgment, you also give yourself a chance to reflect on all the information that you have.

Discover common ground. Ask yourself what things you know about the speaker that the two of you share. Be careful to consider all nonverbal codes—dress, tone of voice, posture, gestures, body movements, and any other mannerisms that may give you more insight into the background, personality, and character of the speaker.

Do not be afraid to remain silent. If you find yourself in the middle of a conversation of which you do not genuinely feel a part, or when you really are not motivated to join, do not try to fake interest by offering thoughtless comments. You are an interesting person in your own right. Defensive or guilty feelings about not taking part in certain conversations will not help you in your efforts to develop empathy, understanding, and clarity.

Listening has its own unique rewards. Not only is it a pleasurable way to pass the time, but you will find yourself becoming a more inviting and interesting speaker because of your experiences.

WORKOUT: IT TAKES THREE

Purpose:	To demonstrate active listening.
Group Size:	Clusters of three participants as size of the room permits.
Time Required:	25 to 40 minutes.
Materials:	None.
Seating Arrangement:	Clusters should be situated in a large room.
Other Considerations:	None.

Process:

1. The trainer-facilitator asks each group of three members to form a circle. Each participant has one turn at playing each of the following roles: speaker, silent listener, and feedback provider.

2. At the beginning of round one, the feedback provider directs questions and comments to the speaker. Questions and comments should be job related. The speaker can answer the questions and address the comments. At this point, the listener is not allowed to speak. A maximum time limit of five minutes should be established.

3. At the end of the first round, the speaker, silent listener, and feedback provider positions rotate to the left, and step 2 is repeated.

4. At the end of the second round, the speaker, silent listener, and feedback provider positions rotate to the left, and step 3 is repeated.

5. At the end of the third round, the trainer-facilitator leads a discussion.

Debriefing Questions:

- Of the three roles, which was the most difficult?
- How well did you listen to the others?
- Were you able to remain interested in the discussion?
- How did you feel about being left out of the conversation?
- When you were being asked questions, what questions were the easiest? What questions were the hardest?
- Did you have difficulty thinking of questions to ask?
- As the speaker, how did you feel about being asked so many questions?
- How can this experience be applied to the team setting?
- How should you approach the team member who neither solicits nor offers feedback?

ROLES

Chapter 20   Friendly Teamwork
Chapter 21   Clash, Bang, Boom!
Chapter 22   The Team that Plays Together Stays Together

Chapter Twenty # Friendly Teamwork

The people we work with can be placed into one of three categories: strangers, associates, or friends. Strangers are those people about whom we know nothing, possibly not even their names. They include new people on the job and those in the company with whom we have no contact. Associates are those people about whom we know just enough information to maintain a working relationship. Friends, on the other hand, are those people whom we know well. Friends share similar backgrounds and interests, are comfortable talking with one another, and share a bond of trust. These categories can be viewed as stages in a relationship. Strangers are the most removed from us while friends are the closest to us. Associates fall somewhere between.

If we could choose our teammates at work, we would probably choose our friends. For example, if a group from work formed a bowling or softball team, our team members would most likely be our friends. Playing on a team made up of our friends has certain advantages. Having more fun is the most obvious advantage. Chances are that the results (team scores) will be better as well. Why? Because, as stated above, friends are people we trust and with whom we are comfortable. Trust allows us to concentrate on our part of the game without worrying about whether our teammates will hold up their end. Implicitly, we know they will.

As a team of friends, we also know the ability and personality of each member. Knowing these attributes helps team members adapt to each player. Making these subtle adaptations helps coordinate the team's efforts.

However, in the workplace, we usually don't have the opportunity to decide who is on our team. This means our team could be composed of strangers and associates as well as friends. To achieve the ideal team, we should turn strangers and associates into friends as quickly as possible.

Specialists in sociology, psychology, and communication have conducted research on the process of making friends. They have observed, for example, that when confronted by a stranger, we are uncertain how he or she will act, and as a consequence, we are uncertain about our own actions. Reducing this uncertainty involves a three-stage process. The first stage is noticing physical appearance, gender, age, and social status. This information is reinforced and clarified with a conversational exchange of personal information. In the workplace, the information shared most likely would include job skills and abilities. Information about the home, family, and hobbies could also be included. During this stage, we are on our best behavior.

In the second stage, we gather information that is personal in nature. Values and beliefs might be shared. During these conversations, we can relax and be less formal. In the final stage, we decide if we enjoyed the interaction up to this point, and we determine if and when to meet again.

After undergoing this process, the person is no longer a stranger but an associate. We now know the abilities and skills that this person will contribute to the team. However, this relationship may still be rather impersonal. Associates are not necessarily our friends. In today's workplace, the term *associates* has replaced employee and taken on special positive value. Associates are co-workers who, although they may not be known enough to be friends, are committed to working cooperatively for the good of the organization. Sometimes associates don't even like each other. Nevertheless, they treat each other with the same respect and helpfulness they have toward customers.

We are attracted to people we perceive to be similar to us. This would mean that for associates to become friends, a lot more information sharing needs to be done. To speed up this process, the focus should be on finding similarities. For example, being parents of school-age children creates a special bond of understanding. Purposely finding and sharing similarities with team members to build mutual understanding accelerates the process of turning strangers and associates into team members who are friends. As mentioned earlier, having friends on our team is the ideal. This doesn't mean it will always be the case, but at least making the effort will be worthwhile.

WORKOUT: INNERVIEW

Purpose:	To reduce uncertainty among teammates.
Group Size:	6 to 12 participants.
Time Required:	25 minutes.
Materials:	None.
Seating Arrangement:	Dyads.
Other Considerations:	Even for long-time friends, getting better acquainted is a worthwhile task.

Process:

1. The trainer-facilitator divides the group into pairs. One participant is designated as A and the other participant as B. Partner A is instructed to ask B a series of questions, which B answers. Questions should be formed around three areas: B's background and hobbies, B's job, and B's beliefs. A maximum time period of five minutes should be established.
2. The process is repeated with partner B asking A the questions.
3. At the end of the exchange, the trainer-facilitator asks the participants to introduce each other to the larger group, emphasizing three things A and B have in common and one unique fact about the other.

Debriefing Questions:

- What thoughts went through your mind during the question-answer session with your partner? Did you want to be understood and appreciated? Were you hesitant about talking about your good points as well as your faults?
- What might you do if you are asked questions deemed too personal?
- What suggestions can you make about turning co-workers who are strangers into associates? Turning associates into friends? Working cooperatively with people you don't like?
- How can natural work groups improve their working relationships?

Chapter Twenty-One

Clash, Bang, Boom!

These sounds, we hope, are not being heard by the members of a team at your workplace. But, if they are, some mending of the team has to be accomplished quickly. Even before you start hearing these awful noises and drawing your sword, the realization of why team members are clashing and the ability to detect these conflicts are necessary.

First, you must realize that everyone has chosen a role within your team. And the nature of "team" is togetherness. This togetherness gets to be too much when certain people only want to be the knight in shining armor, or when tasks seem to be pushed off onto just one person to fight the battle alone. Teamwork turns into tension and sniping.

Second, you must realize that people tend to choose roles based on personality traits. Sometimes, before dividing the work load and determining the tasks, it is almost predictable which person is going to take on which responsibility, who will work well together, or who will take on the least responsibility. Detecting this early will help your team avoid conflict.

To be aware of others' personality traits and avoid these battles, knowing yourself and how others see you is essential. In Chapter Five we discussed the tracks that are ever present in a group. The roles we play pertain to the (*a*) group-orientation roles, which focus on achieving the goal; (*b*) group-relationship roles, which focus on maintaining good relationships among members; and (*c*) self-interest roles, which focus on satisfaction of members' own needs, which do not necessarily pertain to the needs of the group. Thus, personality traits emerge in the roles we play.

Group task roles include initiator, information seeker, energizer, orienter, and secretary.

Group relationship roles include encourager, harmonizer, comedian, gatekeeper, and follower.

Self-interest roles include aggressor, blocker, dominator, deserter, and special-interest pleader.

So the next time you reach down to draw your sword to start a battle, think about the ways to become aware of others. To avoid bloody battles, a smooth and effective teamworking atmosphere composed of different personalities is essential.

Once we are aware of the dynamics at work in our groups, more tasks will get done and fewer lives will be lost.

WORKOUT: ROLL WITH ROLES

Purpose:	To illustrate how personality traits may determine work roles.
Group Size:	Maximum of 15 participants. Others may observe.
Time Required:	20 to 40 minutes.
Materials:	Paper, pencils, a 4" x 6" notecard for each participant with a definition of a role (see Appendix A).
Seating Arrangements:	In a theater-style seating arrangement, all facing the front of the room.
Other Considerations:	Notecards are prepared ahead of time.
Process:	1. Everyone is randomly given a role to perform based on the list that is provided by the trainer-facilitator (see Appendix A).
	2. Everyone is given the following scenario: "You are to imagine that you are a member of a work group. Based on the role you are assigned, complete the task of planning to paint this training room as a person with the traits associated with that role." The group is given 15 minutes to complete this task.
	3. Next, each person jots down who he or she thinks played the roles listed below. The group is given 10 minutes to complete this task.

Role	Person
Initiator	_____
Information seeker	_____
Energizer	_____
Orienter	_____
Secretary	_____
Encourager	_____
Harmonizer	_____
Comedian	_____
Gatekeeper	_____
Follower	_____
Blocker	_____
Aggressor	_____
Dominator	_____
Deserter	_____
Special-interest pleader	_____

Chapter 21 / Clash, Bang, Boom!

Debriefing Questions:

4. After the list has been completed, the trainer-facilitator asks each participant to identify the role he or she played in the group activity and to explain how the role reflects the participant's personality.

5. The trainer-facilitator can lead a discussion, emphasizing that the object of the activity was to create awareness of how others, when taking on different roles based on their personalities, carry out a task.

- What roles were easiest to identify?
- What roles reflected *task-oriented* roles? Describe how these roles surfaced in this activity.
- What roles reflected *relationship-oriented* roles? Describe how these roles surfaced in this activity.
- What roles reflected *self-interest* roles? Describe how these roles surfaced in this activity.
- How did you feel about the seating arrangement? Did anyone propose a different one that is more appropriate for discussion?

Chapter Twenty-Two

The Team that Plays Together Stays Together

Teams are an important part of accomplishing any cooperative activity. However, too often we fail to consider what makes a team. A team is a group of people who work together to accomplish a goal, and all members of a team are needed to achieve its goal. One way in which we can be assured of achieving a goal is by having group members engage in role playing. By engaging in role playing, your team will make itself stronger together.

But what do we mean by the term *role*? Role can be defined as the expectations that others have of an individual. Five roles that are most central to the functioning of a small group are the task leader, the cheerleader, the tension releaser, the information provider, and the devil's advocate.

The *task leader* calls a meeting to order, helps the team stay on track, and steers decision making in the right direction. The *cheerleader* encourages the team, provides pep talks when problems lower morale, and generally works toward establishing a supportive communication climate. The *tension releaser* seeks clarification, calls for time out if tempers flare, and points out that difference of opinion is essential to good decisions. The *information provider* seeks out the expertise of the group, points out facts, and helps the team plan and gather facts. The *devil's advocate* plays the important role of asking "why," urges the team to take time to weigh the possible negative consequences of any decision, and prevents the team from rushing toward disaster.

Civility is the basic ground rule for all role behavior. In transactional language, this is an "I'm O.K., you're O.K." approach. This approach *blames the message for bad news and not the messenger*. This approach embraces an *all for one and one for all* attitude. This approach emphasizes *shared leadership*.

Through self-assessment, you rate your own behavior as a team player. Self-assessment allows you to rate how well you:

- Understand, support, and *own* the team's goals and decisions.
- Listen to everyone on the team.
- Help the team keep on track.
- Cheer the team toward victory.
- Push for fact-based problem solving and decision making.
- Communicate openly and honestly.
- Trust the members of the team.
- Respect differences of opinion.
- Value conflict and diversity.
- Encourage use of the resources of others.
- Play the appropriate role at the appropriate time.

WORKOUT: THE ROLE OF ROLES

Purpose: To acquaint participants with roles group members play.

Group Size: Five participants. Others (up to 20) may observe.

Time Required: 30 to 45 minutes.

Materials: 4" x 6" role-playing notecards (see Appendix E).

Seating Arrangements: At a table. Observers should form a circle around the table.

Other Considerations: Role-playing notecards should be prepared ahead of time. Time should be allotted to allow participants to read the preceding essay.

Process:
1. The trainer-facilitator gives each participant a notecard that describes the role that will be played. Each participant must follow the directions on the notecard.
2. The trainer-facilitator announces that the group, as a whole, needs to develop a list of three ways in which productivity can be increased at their workplace. (Note: If the group is composed of strangers, they may select one person's workplace.) A variation is to have the group follow the same instructions in making the ground rules for a team—possibly their own team. The group is given 15 minutes to complete this task.
3. When the task is completed, the trainer-facilitator asks each participant to write down a few words or phrases that best describe the actions of the other participants (see below).

Role	Behaviors
Task leader	_____
Cheerleader	_____
Tension releaser	_____
Information provider	_____
Devils' advocate	_____

Chapter 22/The Team that Plays Together Stays Together 101

4. After each participant does this, the trainer-facilitator goes around the table, asks each participant to read his or her notecard, and then proceeds with discussion.

Debriefing Questions:
- Did you identify with the role you were playing?
- Which role(s) would you enjoy playing? not playing?
- How important is role playing within a group?
- How does role playing strengthen a group? Weaken a group?
- What advantages do you see with role playing? Disadvantages?
- Which roles were most important in aiding the group in achieving its goals?
- Which roles inhibited the group? Can a group benefit from roles that inhibit the group's performance?
- Are these roles played within your current work groups?
- Which roles should be played at different times by the same person?

DECISION MAKING

Chapter 23 Can This Decision Be Made?
Chapter 24 A Tool Kit for Problem Solving
Chapter 25 When People Agree
Chapter 26 Teamthink

Chapter Twenty-Three
Can This Decision Be Made?

"Decisions, decisions, decisions." Already this morning, I had to decide what to eat for breakfast, whether to bring my umbrella, and where to park—all before I even got to work! Of course, these kinds of decisions are relatively easy to make. Other decisions are not. On the job, as in our personal lives, some decisions we make can have an immense impact on both the organization and our own job performance. In many cases, making a good decision will have important, long-lasting effects.

But how do you know when you have made a good decision? Sometimes it's obvious. With a simple problem, it can be as easy as deciding yes or no. But other times, a problem can be quite complex, with several angles to consider. When you have a complicated problem, how can you be sure you have made the best decision? A good way is to test the decision with the following questions:

- Does the decision solve not only the problem but also the root cause? Is your solution treating the problem or merely the symptoms? In developing a solution that will make a lasting difference, you have to make sure you are not just applying a bandage to a chronic sore spot.

- Does the decision satisfy all the people involved and affected by it? If it is a good decision, it shouldn't interfere with organizational objectives or personal goals. Have you discussed it with the other people who will be involved in its implementation? With their knowledge and support, you will have greater success.

- Can the decision be implemented? You will want to make sure you have taken into account all the time considerations, material problems, human constraints, and other limitations you will encounter in making it work. Clearly, if it can't be done, it's not a good decision.

- Have you thought through all the disadvantages and possible consequences of the decision? Sometimes what looks like a great decision can have unexpected negative results. Have you considered all the alternatives? Make sure you think through all the possible effects of the decision.

If you can answer yes to the questions in the four paragraphs above, then you have a good decision. With the right decision, both you and your team will benefit.

WORKOUT: THE GOOD, THE BAD, THE OTHERS

Purpose: To illustrate the characteristics of "good" and "bad" decision makers.

Group Size: 6 to 12 participants.

Time Required: 40 minutes.

Materials: See The Worst Decision Maker and The Best Decision Maker following in this workout, pencils, two flipcharts, markers.

Seating Arrangement: Groups make own arrangement.

Other Considerations: None.

Process:
1. The trainer-facilitator divides the participants into two groups (group A and group B).
2. The trainer-facilitator tells group A to think of the worst decision makers *each* of them has ever known, and instructs each of them to complete the questions for the "worst decision maker."
3. The trainer-facilitator tells group B to think of the best decision makers *each* of them has ever known, and instructs each of them to complete the questions for the "best decision maker."
4. Both groups are given 10 minutes to complete the questions.
5. After the participants complete their questions, the trainer-facilitator instructs them to share their answers with the other people in their group so they can agree on some general responses for each question to present to the larger group. Each group should use a flipchart to record its conclusions. Both groups are given 10 minutes to complete this task.
6. The trainer-facilitator has a representative from each group present its findings to the larger group. Each group is given 10 minutes to complete this reporting task.
7. The trainer-facilitator leads a discussion if further debriefing is necessary.

The Worst Decision Maker

1. What were (or are) the behaviors and characteristics of the worst decision maker you have ever known?

   _____
   _____
   _____

2. What were your feelings toward this person?

   _____
   _____
   _____

3. What were your behaviors toward this person?

The Best Decision Maker

1. What were (or are) the behaviors and characteristics of the best decision-maker you have ever known?

2. What were your feelings toward this person?

3. What were your behaviors toward this person?

Chapter Twenty-Four

A Tool Kit for Problem Solving

Murphy's law tells us that the one who can smile when things go wrong has thought of someone to blame it on and that information most needed is always the least available. Snafus and frustrations of working life have generated numerous similar cynical observations. Finagle's law concluded that if anything can go wrong, it will, and no matter the result, there is always someone eager to misinterpret it.

You may work in a place referred to as a zoo or a nut factory. It's no wonder our metaphors are mixed. Whitewaters toss us about, we surf turbulent seas, we get caught up in the gears of a machine. Like St. George, it seems you and I are destined to fight the evil dragon and to solve problems rationally when much around us seems irrational.

We hunger for order and structure because we know the frustration of Babel. We are told that teams fail for many reasons: teams do not stay focused on narrowly defined specific problems; teams attack too broad problems; teams have grand solutions; teams blame their problems on others; teams do not have the right tools for problem solving and decision making.

Good solutions are what we want. A good solution must meet two standards: (*a*) it must be of high quality, and (*b*) it must be acceptable to those involved. Therefore, arriving at a good decision hinges on inclusion of those with the necessary expertise and those who must live with a chosen solution. A natural first concern is to define the nature of a problem, whether it be scrap, customer rejects, too much work, or slow delivery time. But before a symptom–cause analysis is undertaken, it is essential that those who are closest to a problem consider *who* should be engaged in its investigation.

A second key issue is *whose* problem is it, and is it really a problem or simply an annoyance? In traditionally managed organizations, many situations are management problems. The situations may be prioritized according to their complexity, how much harm they cause, or by the status of the individual who views the problem. Some of these situations are monkeys on a manager's back. Others are annoyances workers must endure. However, sometimes self-managed teams are best at dealing with task-related problems and may find personnel decisions pertaining to their own people sticky.

Here are some problem-solving decision-making tools that teams should use. They are tools best suited to finding high quality solutions for task-related problems, but they may also improve ownership of solutions.

- For tough problems, *play doctor:* examine the symptoms, locate the extent and seriousness of the pain, take a history of the problem, weigh possible causes, consider alternative remedies, prescribe a cure, and consider the costs.
- For problems that do not need an elaborate investigation, *ask the $64,000 question*. Find the essential question that, if answered, solves the problem.
- For problems that require innovative thinking, try the *if we had our druthers* approach. This approach encourages the group to fantasize about an ideal solution to the problem; after which, it seeks how it might come the closest to making that ideal solution happen.

- For problems that need a creative touch, try *greenlight brainstorming*. Turning on the greenlight makes squelching suggestions taboo. Greenlight says: go, think freely, and obtain as many ideas as possible either though individual or group brainstorming sessions. Save *redlights* and *caution lights* for later meetings.
- For problems that need careful consideration of what might occur if the solution is instituted, assign several team members to *write scenarios*. Team members should be assigned to write a good outcome scenario, a bad outcome scenario, or an unexpected outcome scenario. The team must then determine which scenario is most likely to occur.
- For achieving a particular goal, try *force field* analysis. On a sheet of paper, list the forces that are pushing the group toward goal achievement. On another sheet, list the forces that are restraining goal achievement. After making the two lists, find ways to both strengthen the driving forces and suppress the restraining forces surrounding goal achievement.
- For continuous quality improvement efforts, follow the *plan, test, act sequence*. While gathering information about a problem or a desired goal, we simultaneously develop alternative solutions. The quality movement has formulated several models that facilitate the continuous quality improvement process. The *fishbone*, which diagrams key input variables and key output variables (as described in Chapter Two), is one such model. The *plan, test, act sequence* takes that model into the trial stage and implementation of solutions.

Ford has utilized a *plan, test, act sequence* using an 8D problem-solving process:

D1: Use a team approach.
D2: Describe and verify the problem.
D3: Implement and verify interim (containment) actions.
D4: Define and verify root causes.
D5: Verify corrective actions.
D6: Choose and implement permanent corrective actions.
D7: Prevent recurrence.
D8: Congratulate the team.

CEO Alex Trotman stated, "Teamwork, like commitment, is fundamental if you want to be the best." He likens the 8D process to peeling off layers of an onion to find what really is inside. Notice how *verify* is a word that appears in four of the eight steps.

One of the chief objectives of teamwork training is to familiarize work groups with problem-solving and decision-making tools. Teams soon learn that problem solving is easier if they know how to use the appropriate tool. They also learn that good decisions are matters of finding a consensus—and rarely matters of flipping a coin or voting.

Knowledge and use of some of these various problem-solving tools will do much to put to rest Murphy and Finagle's Laws—laws that belong to the past, not the future.

WORKOUT: JUST DO IT

Purpose: To practice use of team problem-solving tools.

Group Size: Several groups of five to eight participants (not to exceed 40 participants).

Time Required: 60 to 90 minutes.

Materials: Newsprint, markers.

Seating Arrangements: Each group should be seated at a separate table in a large room.

Other Considerations: Natural work groups may use this workout to focus on specific concerns of their work situation. This workout can be conducted at several time periods.

Process:
1. The trainer-facilitator assigns each team a problem such as cutting waste, improving the appearance of the product or service, or improving relationships between adjacent work groups. Teams are given five minutes to identify a problem.

2. The trainer-facilitator instructs each team to follow the 8D problem-solving process described in the preceding essay. Steps D2–D7 should be printed on newsprint. A maximum of 40 minutes is allowed for this step.

3. After the team has finished, each team member must complete the following four-item decision-making process scale:

- Did team members listen to your opinion?

    Not at all   Somewhat   Much   Completely

- Were you able to exert influence over your team members?

    Not at all   Somewhat   Much   Completely

- How satisfied were you with the team decision?

    Not at all   Somewhat   Much   Completely

- How committed were you to the team's decision?

    Not at all   Somewhat   Much   Completely

4. Each team is then given 10 minutes to discuss its answers to the decision-making process scale.

Debriefing Questions:
- What happened during the time allotted for completing steps D2–D7?
- What were considered sound data for verification of the problem, verification of root causes, and verification of corrective action?
- What did you learn about your team members as a result of your team's discussion of the decision-making process scale?
- How might these problem-solving formats be applied to your work setting?

Chapter Twenty-Five

When People Agree

"Let's take a vote." How many times have you heard someone say that? You're part of a group of people who are trying to reach a decision, there are two (or three, or four) different ideas up for consideration, and someone decides it's time to choose which is the best. When we want a decision to be fair, we vote. Right? As members of a democracy, most of us believe that the most equitable, most desirable, most admirable way for a group to reach a decision is by voting. There is a better way.

The better way is known as *consensus decision making*. When decisions are made by consensus, they are even more win-win than decisions reached by a vote. In a vote, one idea wins, but the others lose. When a decision is reached by consensus, no one loses because consensus means everyone in general agrees.

Sounds difficult? Impossible? We all know that one of the few things we can count on at work is that at least one person in the group will disagree with the others. Consensus decision making doesn't claim to change this basic side of human nature. A consensus decision will not necessarily be everyone's first choice. Rather, it is a choice that everyone can support without feeling they are compromising too much.

A consensus decision has to be reached openly. You don't have consensus until a fair hearing is given to all the alternative ideas and they are fully discussed. Each person in the group has to have a chance to express his or her concerns and opinions. Consensus is reached when every person in the group supports an idea (whether they actually prefer it) because the idea is a fair solution and the best idea agreed upon at the time. With consensus, everyone wins because everyone has psychological ownership in the decision.

Making decisions by consensus means encouraging everyone to add to ideas rather than pitting one against the other. Often, combining the input of different people generates a better decision or creative solution. We've all heard that "two heads are better than one." Consensus decision making follows the same principle.

The best aspect of consensus decision making, however, is that when a decision is reached by consensus, it has the support of more people than if it was reached by vote, decree, or flipping a coin. And when you have decisions that people support, you have decisions that work.

See Chapter Thirty Three for the consequences of not involving group members in the decision-making process.

WORKOUT: DECISION BY DESIGN

Purpose: To introduce the concept of consensus decision making.

Group Size: Groups of four to five participants as the size of the room permits.

Time Required: 40 minutes.

Materials: Each group needs three large sheets of white paper, a set of different colored markers, and masking tape.

Seating Arrangement: Groups make own arrangement.

Other Considerations: None.

Process:
1. The trainer-facilitator defines consensus decision making.
2. The participants form groups of four to five people.
3. The trainer-facilitator distributes the materials.
4. The groups are instructed to create a company banner with an original logo. Each group must use all colored markers. The group is allowed 20 minutes to complete the task.
5. The group members hang the banners on the wall where everyone can see them. A representative from each group explains how the banner was created. The trainer-facilitator prompts them to explain how the decisions to choose the colors, the design, and so on were made. From this explanation, the other groups are asked to identify examples of consensus decision making.

Debriefing Questions:
- How did you know when you reached a group consensus on the banner design? On the colors to use?
- How did you deal with group members who disagreed?
- Did each member have a fair hearing or involvement in the group decision?
- How committed do you feel toward the finished banner?

Chapter Twenty-Six

Teamthink

"How could we have been so stupid?" and "What a fiasco!" are prevalent remarks in the phenomenon designated by Irving L. Janis as *groupthink*.

Groupthink refers to the mode of thinking that group members, like us, engage in when agreement seeking becomes so dominant in the group that it overrides a realistic examination of alternative choices. It arises when group members avoid passing harsh judgment on their leader or other members of the group so as not to spoil the cozy "we-feeling" in the group. The syndrome can be blamed for everything from the lack of creativity in an organization (e.g., "A camel is a horse designed by a committee") to delinquent behavior in youngsters (e.g., "My Joey is a good boy; he was just pressured into shoplifting candy bars by his school friends").

Four symptoms have been exhibited by groups that make poor decisions. Victims of groupthink exhibit one or more of these characteristics:

- Unrealistic consideration of alternatives.
- Failure to reexamine initially preferred alternatives or initial alternatives rejected as unsatisfactory.
- Absence of effort to acquire expert testimony.
- Selective bias in the evaluation of information.

Victims of groupthink often share an illusion of being invulnerable, leading them to become overly optimistic and more willing to take risks. They also construct rationalizations to discount any warning signs or negative feedback. They believe in the morality of their group, thus ignoring ethical problems with their decisions.

Victims of groupthink apply pressure to any group member who expresses doubt about the group's decision. They are characterized by a form of self-consensus and minimizing their doubts and the importance of any misgivings. Groupthink victims suffer from a false sense of unanimity. Are those who remain silent really in full agreement with other group members? Finally, the victims assume the role of "mindguards," protecting fellow members and the leader from anything that may disrupt the comfortable feeling in the group.

Teams are even more vulnerable to groupthink than traditional work groups because of the presence of an esprit de corps feeling. Therefore, in the rest of this chapter, we use the term *teamthink*. How can teamthink be prevented when making especially important decisions? Nine recommendations have been developed to aid in the remedy of teamthink:

1. Team members should be assigned the job of *critical evaluator* to encourage members to air objections and doubts.
2. In the beginning of a discussion, the leader should take an impartial position rather than stating favored expectations and personal preferences.
3. External evaluation groups, working on the same problem, should be established.

4. Before a final decision, team members should be encouraged to discuss the problem with outsiders and report reactions to the team.
5. Outside experts, who challenge the team's ideas, should be invited to meetings.
6. At every meeting, one member should play devil's advocate.
7. If a rival team is involved in the decision, the team should assess warning signs from the rival and possibly develop alternative decisions.
8. The team should split into smaller groups, meet separately, discuss the issue, then return to the main team, report new decisions, and deal with any new differences.
9. After a decision is made, a second-chance meeting should be conducted during which every member can rethink issues and doubts before a final decision is made.

The ability to recognize the symptoms and the knowledge of remedies for teamthink enable us to achieve a higher level of team problem solving.

Chapter 26/Teamthink

WORKOUT: THINK, TEAM!

Purpose: To illustrate teamthink.

Group Size: Groups of four to eight participants as the size of the room permits.

Time Required: 30 to 45 minutes.

Materials: Flipchart, newsprint, markers.

Seating Arrangement: Around a table.

Other Considerations: A flipchart or newsprint pad may list the six symptoms and nine recommendations.

Process:

1. The trainer-facilitator explains the concept of teamthink to the participants. The trainer-facilitator outlines the symptoms that lead to the occurrence of teamthink and the recommendations to remedy the problem.

2. The trainer-facilitator initiates a discussion with the team by asking each person to describe a situation in which teamthink occurred.

3. After several examples have been given, the trainer-facilitator reviews the situations with the group and asks it to pick out the symptoms that allowed teamthink to happen.

4. The trainer-facilitator then asks the participants to discuss how they feel teamthink could have been prevented in the given examples.

5. The trainer-facilitator concludes by stressing the importance of becoming aware of the occurrence of teamthink in their work organizations and how it can affect quality decision making.

6. On newsprint, each team makes a sign to alert the group to the dangers of teamthink. All signs should be posted in the room, and participants should circulate around the room to look at the signs.

GOAL SETTING

Chapter 27   Transforming Work into a Vision of LOVE

Chapter Twenty-Seven

Transforming Work into a Vision of LOVE

"I had a vision of love and it was all that you've given to me"

Mariah Carey

As a member of an organization, you are aware that over periods of time, organizations change. But why change? Well, the phrase "don't fix it if it ain't broke" just does not apply anymore in today's business world. The operations that worked effectively yesterday for an organization are all too soon outdated for the world we live in today.

Too often we view change as being bad, negative, or unnecessary. But the truth is that change can be beneficial—provided that people are capable of change. The process of change, which affects the economic, social, and technological environments of our organization, ideally can be defined as *organizational transformation*. During this process, an organization becomes responsible for overhauling its culture.

As your organization undergoes the continual process of development, we are asking you to help create a "vision of LOVE: Learning, Observing, and Validating our Existence." To succeed, we must come together and develop a plan for the future direction of our organization. As you develop your vision, here are some points to consider as we all undergo the same process.

Realize that change can be pleasant! Familiarity breeds security. Yet over 75 percent of American workers state that they could be more effective on the job if things would change! One way in which effectiveness can be increased is through the development of new behavioral patterns or relationships. Remember, we have all learned these patterns and developed new relationships before, so it is possible to do it again! And this task can be accomplished in an easier manner if we adopt a positive outlook. In addition, we can discover and explore new ways of doing things that have not been done before.

Share in the transformation. Don't sit back and ignore the proceedings. Get involved! Transformation, according to Barbara Block, author of *How to Become Happily Employed*, is all about "empowering" the individual. Without you, we cannot make our organization a better place. Keep in mind that our organization is more than the sum of its parts: "individual A + individual B +...". Rather, your organization is a combination of you and your experiences, thoughts, behaviors, and ideas along with everyone else and their experiences, thoughts, behaviors, and ideas.

Understand that transformation takes time. Changing an organization's culture has no quick-fire method. It takes time for change—one conservative estimate is that changing a corporate culture takes between five and ten years. While your organization may not take this much time, keep in mind that any successful organizational change occurs over a period of time. During this time, periods of defining, testing, evaluating, and employing various methods help us determine what is right for the organization and what is right for *you*.

Above anything else, focus on the *people* who compose your work group and organization. By taking these ideas into consideration, you can be part of the team involved in the creation of a vision of LOVE.

See in Chapter Thirty One Chicago Factory Studies, Aircraft Studies, and Harwood Pajama Factory Studies for consequences of conflict between labor and management goals.

Chapter 27/Transforming Work into a Vision of LOVE

WORKOUT: VISION OF LOVE: LEARNING, OBSERVING, AND VALIDATING OUR EXISTENCE

Purpose: To illustrate organizational transformation.

Group Size: Five to seven participants.

Time Required: 50–60 minutes.

Materials: Paper, pencils.

Seating Arrangements: No preference.

Other Considerations: None.

Process:

1. The trainer-facilitator asks the participants to answer the following two-part question. The participants are allowed 10 minutes to complete this task.

- Define the role, as you see it, that you serve within your current workplace or volunteer organization.

_____
_____
_____

- What do you see as being your role in five years?

_____
_____
_____

2. After the 10-minute time limit has expired, the trainer-facilitator asks each participant to briefly share his or her responses. This sharing should take no more than 15 minutes.

3. The trainer-facilitator asks the participants to answer the following two-part question. Participants are allowed 10 minutes to complete this task.

- After listening to the other participants, define the role that your group serves within your organization.

_____
_____
_____

- What do you see as being this group's role in five years?

_____
_____
_____

4. The trainer-facilitator asks each participant to briefly share his or her responses. This sharing should take no more than 15 minutes. Sharing may need to be selective based on the number of participants.

Debriefing Questions:
- How will change affect your role in the organization?
- How might your organization change during the next 5 to 10 years?
- How will others in the organization be affected by this change?
- What is the commonality among the group members' vision of the future?

THE NONVERBAL ELEMENT

Chapter 28 Space: The Final Frontier
Chapter 29 The Smile Doesn't Mean I'm Happy

Chapter Twenty-Eight

Space: The Final Frontier

Have you ever heard children saying to each other, "This is my side. This is your side. Stay on your own side!" Well, it may sound like a childish thing to do, but look around, because the acorn doesn't fall far from the tree. These same messages are displayed in your workplace through nonverbal communication.

Why is the chief executive's office often on the top floor with an expansive view, while others merely have cubicles? Why do workers complain about cramped quarters in a building that has to hold too many people with too little space? These questions and thoughts all pertain to the communication concept called *proxemics, proximity,* or more simply, *space*.

Glass-mirrored buildings alongside a Dallas freeway; giant skyscrapers in the canyons of Wall Street; massive sculptures in a pastoral landscape and winding drive into North Carolina's Research Triangle; a blistering hot, deafening, four story, two-block-long open space, filled with furnaces and overhead cranes enclosed by blackened walls and ceilings in Gary—each is a place of work with a very loud message. Like the pyramids of ancient Egypt, massiveness and richness tell us of wealth. Most corporate headquarters are designed to read as signatures of power.

How a workplace is constructed affects the relationships of those within it. You like to have your own space. Why? Your elbows aren't bigger than anyone else's. It has to do with status. Larger space and privacy nonverbally communicate higher status. Whether a large or small company, proximity is virtually as important as every other communication concept, and they all relate to teamwork. How? The awareness of the messages conveyed with proximity and the ability to read those nonverbal cues enable the flow of communication to run smoothly without workers having to verbally mark their boundaries.

The importance of an employee is nonverbally communicated through space of the actual office (per square feet the office measures) as well as the distance or location from the superior's office. During your first week or so at a new company, these cues may help make your adjustments less stressful.

Barriers, such as doors and partitions, help establish the lines that may or may not be crossed. For example, a manager of an organization usually has an office in the back, farthest from the door to the public. This shows status. Clerical workers usually have offices or cubicles near the executive secretary's and the manager's office. Often workers move closer and closer to the manager's office as the level of status increases. Immediate supervisors usually are closest to the manager's office.

It must be stressed that this is a usual but not an absolute way to arrange an organization. It is most often found in a structure similar to what was just described. Teamness tends to democratize the space in a workplace. Status gives way to getting the job done. Barriers give way to seeing co-workers from other departments more frequently in your own work area. Teamness flattens organizations. Some of the trends that will reshape the workplace, according to *Fortune,* are in keeping with the team way:

- The average company will become smaller, employing fewer people.
- The traditional hierarchical organization will give way to a variety of different forms, including the formation of networks of specialists.
- The vertical division of labor will be replaced by a horizontal division.
- The paradigm of doing business will shift from making a product to providing a service.

So the next time you start a new job or are promoted in your current organization, stop to think about whether you should expect the office on the top floor with the windows and a swivel chair. These concepts may not be blatantly told to you. You just may be able to shape the space of your future!

See Chapter Thirty Two for examples of importance of space in forming work groups.

Chapter 28/Space: The Final Frontier

WORKOUT: DO NOT CROSS

Purpose: To create awareness of nonverbal cues conveyed through proxemics.

Group Size: 10 participants.

Time Required: 20 to 30 minutes.

Materials: Unequal size pieces of rope or thick string (a minimum of four feet in length) for each participant, status cards (see Appendix F).

Seating Arrangements: Large empty room.

Other Considerations: This workout is more appropriate for workers in office settings.

Process:
    1. The trainer-facilitator randomly gives each participant a status card and a piece of rope.
    2. The trainer-facilitator announces to the group members that with their ropes and based on their status, they must outline their office or work space, making a circle or square on the floor, making the maximum area the length of the rope. They must confer with their co-workers to establish the best use of space. The trainer-facilitator also announces that the maximum total space of the company is the training room floor itself. The group is given 15 minutes to complete the task.

Debriefing Questions:
- How much space, based upon your role, did you feel you deserved?
- How did your co-workers feel about your decision?
- Are there unwritten rules for some of the space? How did you come to learn these rules? Did you want to change these rules? Why?
- What nonverbal messages were sent through the territorial office space you established?
- If this space could speak, what would it say about the office space configurations your team made?
- How did you negotiate the size of your work space?
- Why did you select the space you selected?
- If changes were made in the space allocations (making all space equal), how would that affect communication among organizational members?

Chapter Twenty-Nine

The Smile Doesn't Mean I'm Happy

How many times have you seen a facial expression of a co-worker that did not reflect what was being said verbally? These messages can be interpreted in so many different ways. The key is to be aware of facial expressions and the cues that communicate the real or intended messages.

Nonverbal cues can either override a message or convey it more accurately. Why? Because more thought tends to be put into a verbal message, whereas a nonverbal message expresses emotions and reflects a person's feelings.

Different parts of the face tend to display different emotions. Scholars in the field of communication divide the face into three parts: forehead and eyes, cheeks and nose, and mouth and chin. Each part contributes to our facial display of feelings and emotions.

To better communicate and create a teamwork atmosphere, we all must *face* the same direction. This includes understanding how interpreting another person's feelings is often based on common facial expressions. This awareness is necessary for a smooth running work atmosphere.

Several different emotions are exhibited in the vocal tone of co-workers. These include anger, disgust, happiness, sadness, interest, surprise, contempt, fear, determination, and bewilderment. Stop for a moment and think about, perhaps even act out, what each of these emotions would look like. Are some of them similar in the actual facial expression or movement? Are they vastly different?

Differences exist in some of the meanings of the facial expressions, but so do similarities in formations of the facial muscles that display them. Thus, we must take special care in deciphering these nonverbal messages. Co-workers can tell us what nonverbal message we are sending and if our nonverbal cues complement or contradict our verbal message.

Most important, we need to consider that *not* all nonverbal facial expressions are interpreted in exactly the same way. In fact, some people may not realize they "look disgusted" because sometimes those emotions leak out. Checking our perceptions is just as important for nonverbal cues as it is for the words we hear.

WORKOUT: A SMILE OR A FROWN?

Purpose: To create awareness of the nonverbal messages displayed through facial expression.

Group Size: Even number of participants.

Time Required: 20 minutes.

Materials: Each dyad needs one set of statement cards (see Appendix G), pencils, and two sets of emotion cards (see Appendix G).

Seating Arrangements: Dyads.

Other Considerations: This workout may not be appropriate for groups governed by traditional sex-role stereotypes.

Process:
1. Participants sit facing a partner, preferably someone with whom they are not familiar.
2. Partner A is given the statement notecards and one set of the emotion notecards. The trainer-facilitator tells A to relay the messages on the statement notecards, using the various emotions listed on the second notecard.
3. Partner B is given the other set of the emotion notecards. The trainer-facilitator tells B to listen to the statements made by A and, using the emotion notecards, identify the emotion(s) used by A in each of the statements.
4. The trainer-facilitator may then lead a discussion using the following debriefing questions.

Debriefing Questions:
- Which emotions were easily identifiable?
- Which emotions were not easily identifiable?
- Are emotions more easily identifiable through verbal statements or through facial expression?
- What nonverbal clues allowed you to decipher the appropriate emotion?

PART III
ROOTS OF WORK GROUP RESEARCH

Chapter Thirty

Pioneering Work Group Research: The 1920s and 1930s

OUR LEGACY OF GROUPS IN THE WORKPLACE

From the pioneering efforts of early researchers of groups in the workplace we have come to learn more about organizational man as a social being. These early efforts, when viewed together, give us a rich picture of the effects of groups in the workplace. Viewed in isolation, they are subject to much criticism for faulty methodology, poor analyses, research biases and the like. But each lays down an important block of knowledge, which if examined together, can tell us much about groups in the organizational setting.

These pioneer researchers have given us a legacy—a history of organizational man. Thus, like all history, if examined carefully and closely and in a different time and space, it can tell us much, not so much from what the researchers say but from what they fail to say or see. It is our intent to share with you some of these early works and to highlight important research efforts so that we can learn about group behavior in organizational settings. Collectively, these studies, like collections of individuals, become greater than their individual contributions.

Groups in the workplace have been studied by many researchers from a variety of disciplines, each analyzing a slightly different aspect of the life of small groups in the workplace. Consider the following pioneers and their fields of study: Elton Mayo and the researchers from Harvard University in the field of industrial psychology and later human relations; E. W. Bakke and Charles Walker in psychology; Kurt Lewin in group dynamics; George Homans in sociology; J. L. Moreno and other sociometrists; Eliot Chapple, William Whyte and Conrad Arensberg in applied social anthropology or interactionism; and Daniel Katz, Stanley Seashore, and others in social psychology.

To place early research in perspective, it is important for us to understand what was going on in business and industry at that time. In the late 1800s and early 1900s, managers were looking for ways to encourage workers to be more productive and profitable for the company. This is not unusual even today; however, at this time emphasis was not on the organization of groups to enhance productivity and profits, but rather to look at the structure of the organization. Emphasis, therefore, was on organizational structure rather than the work group. This should not be thought of as a criticism of early management, as they were merely attending to necessary functions given the conditions of their time and knowledge of organizational man.

Frederick W. Taylor appeared to provide many of the answers early managers were searching for through a scientific method of managing workers. In 1899, he had already organized his own firm to introduce scientific management principles to industrial organizations. Taylor's book, *Principles of Scientific Management,* published in 1911, presented his views on human labor and methods of organizing workers to be more productive, hence, more profitable to themselves and management. It was in this book that we find a view accepted by many about the effects of groups in the workplace.

Taylor argued that jobs should be individualized because group influences restrict worker output. He stated:

When workmen are herded together in gangs, each man in the gang becomes far less efficient than when his personal ambition is stimulated . . . when men work in gangs, their individual ambition falls almost invariably down to or below the level of the worst man in the gang . . . they are pulled down instead of being elevated by being herded together. (p. 73)

Taylor described the work group and its influence on output or production as "systematic soldiering," that is, group control over the methods of working and the level of output and earnings to produce below the expectations of management (Lupton, 1966, p. 50). Thus, Taylor's solution to this problem was to pay careful attention to the "formal organization" and the division of labor. Supervision should be tight, he concluded, to assure adherence to company production norms, and managers should appeal to the economic motives of the workers to see that these norms were met. Taylor believed this would offset the effects of the work group on individual performance.

This view of organizational man is known as Theory X and it was the dominant perception of men in the workplace during this time. It was not until the 1920s that the effects of groups in the workplace began to be recognized and examined, although this was done indirectly. The first recognition of the "human component" in industrial organizations is attributed to Elton Mayo and his research associates at Harvard University.

PHILADELPHIA TEXTILE MILL

Elton Mayo from Harvard University gave us our first major study of industrial workers in the early 1920s. He examined the effects of employee working conditions at the Philadelphia Textile Mill, more specifically, the Mule Spinning Department. He reported the findings in the 1924–25 Journal of Personnel Research, volume 3.

Mayo was "historically the first person to make studies of industrial behavior in which insights and methods from the functional school of social anthropology were combined with those from clinical psychology" (Arensberg, 1951, p. 336). As a clinical psychologist, Mayo was concerned with the physiological effects of work conditions on workers of the Mule Spinning Department. He was influenced by functional anthropologists, Malinowski and Radcliffe-Brown, "who were reworking the area of ethnology as a function of social life and customs for all men and all human groups" (Arensberg, 1951, p. 337).

When Mayo arrived at the plant, he found the following problems: low output, high turnover, fatigue, and low morale. Mayo diagnosed these conditions as "anomie," a concept developed by the sociologist Durkheim. Mayo believed the solution to these problems was to give the workers a means of venting their feelings and frustrations and to permit them to determine when they should take their rest periods or work breaks. He felt that this would combat fatigue and give them opportunities for rest. Mayo had a nurse serve as a "listening post" for the workers and their problems. He concluded that the workers' opportunity to talk out their problems with the nurse resulted in an increased number of social relationships among the group members, the improvement of morale, reduction in the turnover rate, and reduction of fatigue through the rest pauses.

Arensberg (1951) rightly pointed out what Mayo failed to see—that the changes were a result of alterations in the basic working relationship among workers and their environment. The workers had more say over changes in their environment such as deciding when they could take their rest pauses. When a new supervisor took this responsibility away from the workers, the previous problems reoccurred, nurse or no nurse! This case demonstrates, according to Arensberg, the "dependence of morale and performance upon basic interpersonal relationships in the dynamics of small group behavior" (1951, pp. 338–39). This study further demonstrated that workers like to have control over their environment. The mere presence of other work group members, however, is not enough, nor is interaction enough to enhance morale and improve productivity. Being in *control* of one's fate through the dynamic collectivity of the small work group is what matters to workers.

According to Arensberg (1951), Mayo's examination of worker-to-worker relations resulted in the birth of the "doctrine of information organization or teamwork" (p. 339). Teamwork is a word that has grown in significance and importance since that time. The influence of the work team and the importance of being a team player can be seen in the results of the now famous Hawthorne Experiments conducted at the Western Electric Company.

HAWTHORNE EXPERIMENTS

While Mayo was completing his research at the textile mill, employees of the Western Electric Company's Hawthorne works collaborated with the National Research Council in studying the effects of lighting on worker productivity. From 1924 to 1927, the NRC carried out the "illumination studies." According to Mayo (1946), no official report was published, but the experiment involved the study of two work groups. Each group was placed in a separate room segregated from each other and the rest of the workers in the plant. One group served as the control group and the other as the experimental group. In the experimental condition, researchers lowered the lighting intensity and varied the rest periods by certain amounts and then measured the output of the workers during each period. Much to the experimenters' surprise, there were no significant output differences between the control and experimental work groups, but both groups had an increase in production.

In follow-up experiments, workers were allowed to believe that the illumination was being increased during one period and decreased during another period, although in fact it was not. There was no change in output, although there was some complaint during the supposed low-light condition. It was not until the illumination was in fact decreased to the level of moonlight in yet another test condition that production declined.

These unexpected findings were later explained as due to experimenters who were "screwy" because they had obtained only production output curves and no human motivational data (Roethlisberger, 1941).

In April 1927, Elton Mayo and his research associates from the Department of Industrial Research at Harvard University were asked to conduct experiments at the Hawthorne Works. Mayo was anxious to further test rest pauses or work breaks in a different setting. The Harvard group conducted a series of experiments and intensive interviews with the workers over a five-year period from 1927 through 1932.

The first experiments were conducted with women workers in the relay assembly test room from April 1927 to June 1929 under the direction of Mayo's assistants, Roethlisberger and Dickson. This involved 13 experimental periods. They reported a continual increase in workers' output throughout the periods under study regardless of the piece rate pay plan in effect or the length of work pauses. Mayo (1946) concluded, "This upward trend has continued too long to be ascribed to an initial stimulus from the novelty of starting a special study" (p. 67). Roethlisberger and Dickson (1939) described changes in the relations of the women with each other. There was an increase in their awareness of themselves as a group separated from other women with whom they had worked in the large assembly work room.

According to M. L. Putnam of Western Electric, "... the best way to improve morale was through improved supervision" (Mayo, 1946, p. 77). Sofer (1972), however, offered another explanation for the results of the relay assembly test room:

> The only constant set of factors in these periods were the existence of the small social group, the relatively high stability in its membership, the feelings of mutual loyalty the women developed to each other as the experiment continued, and the special treatment of the group by management, that is, their being selected for participation in the experiment and being consulted before each change was introduced. (p. 67)

With this line of reasoning, one can explain the reactions of the women as an adaptation to their changing environment. How did the women respond to the constant changes in their work environment and working conditions? They turned to each other. Group membership was the only constant in their changing work world. The environment literally facilitated the feeling of loyalty and esprit de corps among the group members. The environment affected their activities with each other and their expressed sentiments in a positive manner, which was reflected in their increased output. This, coupled with the ability of the workers to express their opinions about the changes that were introduced in their work environment, explains the increase in productivity. Yet another explanation for working faster was that workers in the relay test room were given daily reports about how many relays they assembled. Immediate feedback is important to workers (Schacter, 1989; Whitsett & Yorks, 1983).

The second set of experiments began in August of 1928 in the mica splitting test room and in November of that same year in the second relay assembly test room. These experiments yielded similar results as before. In November of 1931, the last series of studies were conducted in an effort to explain the results from the previous experiments on increased worker productivity. This was the bank wiring room experiment involving 14 men. The men were placed in a separate room comparable to the working conditions in the plant. There was no experimental manipulation this time, only an observer. Interviews were also conducted for this study.

Interestingly, these men did *not* increase their output. In fact, they operated below the company standard. The company set the standard at 2½ equipments or 6,600 connections per day; however, the group standard was 2 equipments or 6,000 connections per day. As Homans pointed out, this could hardly be viewed as restriction of output because it was not an objectively low effort (1950, p. 60). As Sofer (1972) explained, there was a "belief ... expressed in the group that to exceed this standard would in some way ... be dangerous" (p. 69). This is a situation where the work group's goals directly conflicted with management set goals. The group had a production norm and very strict rules and rituals to assure that no member went beyond the group norm or below it. As Homans pointed out, those who exceeded the group production norm were chastised by the group and called "speed kings"; those who deviated from the group standard output were called "chiselers." They also created a game to force the members to comply to the work group norm called "binging." Co-workers would "bing" (hit) another on the arm to signal when they were working too fast.

These findings from the Hawthorne experiments point to the strong influence of the work group. The workers believed that two equipments per day was a fair day's work in exchange for the pay they were receiving. When these men were interviewed and asked about their output, they gave the following explanations for their lower-than-company-norm performance: (*a*) fear of unemployment by working themselves out of a job if production was too high, (b) fear of management raising the standard output performance norm, (c) protection of the slower worker, and (d) satisfaction on the part of management. No one was being reprimanded for the current rate of output, so why change?

We also find in the bank wiring room that the internal environment and the spatial arrangements of the workers were such that they facilitated the emergence of two cliques, each with its own productivity norms (Smith, 1973, p. 51). Homans also explained that each clique had its own "games" and activities to assure the group would comply to the work group production norms.

Seashore (1954) summarized the major conclusions of the Hawthorne study this way:

- The primary group formation takes place even if it is not formally accepted or encouraged by management.
- The formation of the primary group associations may conflict with rather than coincide with the formal organizational plan.
- The primary group formation seems to be facilitated by the interactions required by the work process and the work environment.
- The productivity and behavioral standards are determined by the informal group through consensus, and they develop a system to assure that they are enforced. (pp. 5–6)

The findings of Mayo and his associates completely upset the traditional view of Taylor's scientific management philosophy accepted and followed by so many at the time—that workers are motivated to produce by economic incentives and the work group affects production adversely. The Hawthorne Study was plagued with methodological problems. For example, slower, overtalkative women workers in the relay test room were replaced, and depressed workers were discharged, leading to fear of job loss. Therefore, this fear of job loss, and not the motivation of workers, may explain the productivity levels. Despite all the methodological problems with the Hawthorne experiments, they did demonstrate the importance of small groups in the workplace.

THE ABC SHOE FACTORY

In 1938, a study was undertaken to examine the role of teamwork in a shoe factory. This was part of a research course under the direction of Eliot Chapple. Alexander Horsfall from the College of Business Administration at the University of Florida became a participant-observer at the ABC Shoe Factory from July 12 to August 13, 1938. Conrad Arensberg, Chairperson of the Department of Sociology at Barnard College, took the original paper written by Horsfall and rewrote and reevaluated the observations he recorded (see Horsfall & Arensberg, 1949).

This project was a pioneer effort, as its purpose was to "describe and measure the interaction within groups of shoe company workers" (Horsfall & Arensberg, 1949, p. 13). The theoretical grounding for this study was based on the philosophy of anthropologists Chapple, Coon, Arensberg, Whyte, and others who described themselves as "interactionists." Arensberg (1951) explained this philosophy:

> Group life is an outcome of interaction. These interactions are events of stimulation and response between one and the next taking place in time. (p. 344)

The interactionists made the following observations: (a) they identified and enumerated the actors (workers); (b) they established the order of activity among the actors/workers; and (c) they put their observations into a time sequence. Using this format the researchers attempted to prove quantitatively the existence of the "informal organization" of the *work group* and its influence on worker output and behavior in organizations.

Horsfall observed four teams in the bottoming room of the shoe factory. As a participant-observer, he monitored the interaction among these workers by recording who initiated and received the interaction and the time sequence of events. In addition to these notations, he and his research team interviewed the work teams. The results revealed that while members interacted within their own work team to varying degrees, only a few members had high ratings of interaction. There was frequent interpersonal activity within the work groups, showing that they communicated most frequently with one another as opposed to communicating with workers outside their teams. Examination of this "in-team" interaction revealed that the talk centered around only one or two members who were highly interactive, and all activities were structured around them. The researchers concluded that the spatial position and personality of the members were some explanations for why they were selected as team leaders. It is interesting to note that the informal leaders of two teams were the oldest and the most experienced male workers (Horsfall & Arensberg, 1949, p. 22).

The subjective or interview data analysis of the ABC Shoe Factory supported the findings of other studies of small group behavior in the workplace. That is, the natural work groups at this factory set up an informal system to allocate work load, equalized the pay of work team members, and spread out and apportioned the rest periods/breaks among the work team members. This was all done *outside* the norms set by management and despite the incentive piece rate system—causing another blow to the economic theory of motivating workers established by Taylor.

Workers at the shoe factory developed an elaborate coding system to let each team member know where he or she was in the production scheme and when to speed up or slow down. They communicated this by placing a certain object on a team member's chair. Each object meant something to the workers, but was not obvious to outsiders. With these objects, they were able to communicate to each other when they needed to speed up the production, slow down, or take a break. This system was designed as an attempt to equalize the work-flow process among team workers—a system that was inherently unequal, as some jobs in the shoe factory were easier than others.

The significance of the results from the ABC Shoe Factory rests in the behavior of the work teams. They recognized each other through their interactions or lack of interactions. They developed a system by which collectively they could take control of their work environment and establish an equitable pay system for all, in spite of their individual losses. When the team won, they all won!

SUMMARY

The studies just reported came from different types of industries in different geographical areas. Although the researchers approached the study of work groups through different perspectives, they did have several things in common. They all recognized the value and importance of groups within the workplace. They all demonstrated that informal or not, groups do exist and flourish in the industrial setting. Groups are formed as a result of conditions of the workplace environment and/or the work process itself. These groups create norms that dictate the performance behaviors of their members. This, at times, means an increase in output or productivity, and at other times, it leads to restriction in output. These norms were agreed upon by work group members, and compliance was achieved through ostracism or games. We also found that social interaction influenced the "group spirit," but interaction was *not* necessarily related to production. In addition, we found that when group members believed that the standards set by management were not equitable, safe, or appropriate, the group would create its own standard based on the philosophy "a fair day's work for a fair day's pay."

Chapter Thirty-One

Work Group Action Research in the 1940s

In the 1940s, research centered around the effects of groups on restriction of output and on the rate of absenteeism and turnover. The research studies to follow are representative of the type of research efforts of that time.

THE CHICAGO FACTORY STUDIES

In a 1946 article in *Applied Anthropology*, Orvis Collins, Melville Dalton, and Donald Roy presented the results of their lengthy investigation of several factories in the Chicago area. The report was prepared for the Committee on Human Relations in Industry at the University of Chicago. The research took place between 1940 and 1945 (Collins, Dalton, & Roy, 1946). They attempted to answer the following research question: "Why do many work groups consistently practice regulated restriction of output in disregard of what appears to be the economic advantage of the individual involved?" (Collins et al., 1946, p. 13)

To answer this question, the researchers examined three factories using participant-observation techniques. For six months, Orvis Collins became a heavy machine operator and conducted extensive interviews with the workers in one plant. Over a four-year period, Melville Dalton was an incentive engineer for a factory. During an 11-month period, Donald Roy served as a drill press operator while observing workers at another factory.

From these three researchers' observations and direct experiences with workers and the workplace, they attempted to explain why restrictions occurred in the plants they studied. One explanation found was in the perceptual differences between management and the workers on what constituted a "fair day's work." Both parties agreed that workers should give management a fair day's work, but they disagreed on just what that meant. The incentive engineers set the production standard, that is, how many units should be produced during a given period of time. These standards were based on economic incentives in the hope of offsetting group production norms. However, the workers did not agree with this company standard. They did not believe that the amount of effort they had to expend to achieve the standard was worth the pay they were getting in return. When work groups agreed on what *they* believed was a fair day's work, they set up a system to enforce *their* standard. The effectiveness of the work group in forcing other workers to comply is evident when one examines the number of workers who did not comply or conform to the groups' pressures.

In factory A, out of 50 workers, there were no workers who did not conform to the group standard; in factory B, out of 90–110 workers, only four were consistently not conforming to the group norm; and in factory C, out of 200 workers, 10 did not yield to group pressures. It is interesting to note that some older workers were permitted by the group to produce beyond the group standard. As Collins et al. pointed out, this special allowance might have been permitted because older workers should be able to perform faster because they have more experience. But newcomers were not given this permission because they would make the other workers look bad.

Thus, when a newcomer first entered the factory, he was confronted with a conflict in the production norms of management and his co-workers. Each group attempted to persuade the newcomer to produce at the group rate. Collins found that one superintendent used poetry and morality stories to appeal to the worker's sense of moral obligation and individuality of spirit. The following is an excerpt from a worker's diary:

> He [the shop superintendent] told me about what he considered the importance of getting in with the right people at the beginning and drew a folder out of his desk from which he read a poem about thinking. The title of the poem was something about "if we only think." The thesis of the poem was that if we give thought to each of our daily actions we get along better with other people. He then read an essay, "The Crooked Stick," which appeared to have been clipped from some advertising matter. The thesis of the essay was that there are crooked sticks in every woodpile, and that they are more trouble than they are worth. He said he thought it would be a good thing if we could find out some way to make those people who are trouble makers see that being trouble makers is not to their advantage. (Collins et al., 1946, p. 3)

The work groups also used techniques to indoctrinate the newcomer into their beliefs. They would set up "morality plays" using a nonconformist as representative of what would happen to this newcomer if he did not conform to the group's norms. Look closely at the conversation between two older workers:

Ed

> That guy (pointing to a machine) is the greatest rate buster in the shop. Give him a job he can make a nickel on and he'll bust his ass for the company.

Mike

> That's no lie. He's ruined every job on that machine. They've cut him down to the point where he has to do twice the work for half the pay. A few more like him would ruin this shop.

Ed

> It's guys like that that spoil the shop for the rest of us. Somebody ought to take a piece of babbit and pound some sense into his thick skull. That's the only kind of treatment a guy like that understands.

Mike

> We're handling him the best way as it is. The only way to handle those bastards is not to have a thing to do with them. That guy hasn't got a friend in the place and he knows it. You can bet your life he thinks about that every time he comes to work. (Collins et al., 1946, p. 9)

This was all staged for the benefit of the newcomer. Before newcomers were accepted as members of the work group, they were tested to assure that they would conform to the group's production standard. If the new hires did not fit in, the regular workers would withhold essential information the new employees needed to perform their jobs effectively. In addition, older workers would give new workers who ignored the group's norms the worst jobs and would ostracize them both on and off the job.

With such strong pressure to conform to the group's production standard, we may wonder why some members of the factory did not conform. In an effort to explain the motivation for the nonconformist behavior, Dalton examined the personal backgrounds of these workers. He found that there was a fundamental difference in the attitude and belief systems between high performers who were the conformers and those who were nonconformers. Superficial analysis showed that the nonconformists came from a rural background, were politically anti-New Deal, and most were anti-union. These nonconformists had a strong work ethic—they believed that it was their moral obligation to work as hard as they could. That is, the support for their beliefs and values was greater than the pressure exerted by the group to conform. They could not and would not adopt values and beliefs that were inconsistent with their own.

Collins et al. (1946) summarized the findings of their research in the following manner: (a) restriction of output reflects status conflict between "office and shop"; (b) restriction of output is an expression of resentment toward management-instituted controls; and (c) restriction of output is an "expression of a cleavage in social ethics" (p. 13). In short, those who held down their production believed pressures by management were unjustified.

THE AIRCRAFT STUDIES

In 1944, Mayo and Lombard reported the results of their investigations of the aircraft industry in southern California. They looked at teamwork and its effect on labor turnover and absenteeism in that industry. They found that "the highest incidence of absences and terminations is among those who are new to their work or to the plant, and who have not worked themselves into relationship with the job and with their fellow workers" (Sofer, 1972, p. 70).

Mayo and Lombard explored the company's work centers, which were defined as individuals working side by side every day on a common or similar task (Sofer, 1972). Mayo and Lombard found that work centers with the lowest rate of absenteeism and turnover were ones that had a "lead man" who was employee centered and who helped the newcomers fit into the work group and the work system. The successful lead men were ones who helped new members assimilate into the system.

A lead man had a link to his fellow workers through his activities done on their behalf. For example, one lead man with low absenteeism thought he had three major activities to perform: (a) to help his fellow workers in whatever way he could, (b) to adjust technical difficulties for the workers, and (c) to handle worker contact with the time study men, inspectors, department foremen, and others in the plant for the members. The lead men also were accepted by management because it was management who had placed them in that position. Thus, the lead men "deliberately planned and executed assimilation of individuals into the social system of the plant." This, Mayo and Lombard concluded, resulted in low turnover in that lead man's work unit (Seashore, 1954).

We find that a worker's behavior was a result of the work group members' acceptance because of the significant actions of a leader. Mayo and Lombard explained, "If the worker did not feel respected by management and linked with it through personal relationships or through some symbol or agency of management, there tended to be a lower contribution, reinforced by teammates sharing the same sentiments" (Sofer, 1972, p. 71). In looking over the results of their studies of groups in the workplace, Mayo and Lombard were impressed with the "invariable persistence of the human desire for active association in teamwork with others" (Sofer, 1972, p. 72).

THE HARWOOD PAJAMA FACTORY STUDY

The Harwood manufacturing company had an extensive history of attempting to apply social science approaches to the solution of its problems. Alfred Marrow, president of Harwood, sought the advice and counsel of Kurt Lewin, Alex Bavelas, and John R. P. French. Kurt Lewin, the psychologist who helped develop the field of group dynamics, became a very influential force during the years of experimentation at Harwood. His philosophy of groups and his theoretical orientation of field theory served as the basis for the research (Coch & French, 1948).

In a visit to the Harwood plant in 1944, Lewin suggested to Dr. Marrow that one reason for the high rate of turnover may have been that the workers were under too much pressure to produce. Lewin proposed that the firm stop putting pressure on the women to produce and show them that it was possible to reach their performance quota without strain. The company brought in 60 highly skilled and experienced operators to serve as models/trainers.

Workers were encouraged to set their own performance goals, and trainers were asked to aid them in setting realistic attainable goals. They were also asked to give the workers encouragement and not criticize their work. Marrow proudly reported at a convention, "As a result of the change in goals and reduction in the time allowed to achieve the easier goals, the turnover rate dropped 50 percent for the entire plant" (French & Coch, 1948, p. 473). Apparently when the workers saw that the quota was attainable, they began to realize they could achieve that work level. Thus, through social comparison and the dynamic interaction of the work group, these workers increased their production.

The Harwood Company later commissioned Alex Bavelas to conduct a series of experiments in an effort to explain worker behavior. Bavelas studied the effects of giving a group of employees more control over their output and engaging them in goal setting. Bavelas discovered that when the workers set their own production rates they maintained the level of performance *they* set for five months. Bavelas then wanted to see the effects of discussion on worker productivity when they were not able to set their own performance rate. He found only a small increase in output.

In another experiment, Bavelas introduced the concept of increased self-management to the workers. Two groups were paid on a piece-rate basis with a minimum output required. One group was permitted to plan its own hourly and daily level, the other group was not. The group permitted to plan its own rate raised production to a higher level and maintained this level, while the other group's remained unchanged (Sofer, 1972). This suggests that economic motives may not necessarily be the driving force for increased productivity.

Bavelas was succeeded by John R. P. French, who in turn worked with Lewin doing research at the pajama factory. One of the most serious problems faced by the Harwood Company was getting workers to adapt to changes in the work methods and jobs so necessary to compete in the garment industry. Therefore, French was called in to see what Harwood could do to overcome this resistance on the part of the workers to change. French was aided in this endeavor by Lester Coch, personnel manager at Harwood (Sofer, 1972).

The major research questions were: (a) why do people resist change so strongly? and (b) what can be done to overcome this resistance? The theoretical base for understanding why people resist change rests in the philosophy of Kurt Lewin. According to Lewin's force field theory, whenever people are placed in a new situation, they need to confront two opposing forces—driving and restraining. The driving forces aid a person in accepting the changing situation because the person can see reasons for making the desired change. The restraining forces are those things that reinforce the person's desire to have things remain the way they are or to resist change in the environment.

Whenever women in the manufacturing company changed to another job, they had to relearn or retrain to get to their previous performance levels. The small compensation in their paychecks for making the job change was too little for what they had to go through to meet the accepted production standard. That is, the restraining forces were greater than the driving forces. The researchers were interested in learning if *participation* in decisions pertaining to these new changes would lessen resistance to change and hence reduce the workers' restraining forces. Three experimental conditions were created:

1. Thirteen pajama folders were involved in participation through representation in designing the changes made in their jobs.
2. Two groups of seven or eight pajama examiners participated totally in designing the changes made to their jobs.
3. A control group of hand pressers were observed as they went through the usual factory routine when their jobs were changed.

The results of the experiment indicated that the control group with no voice in the job changes developed resistance to change immediately. They expressed aggression toward management and hostility against their supervisors by deliberately restricting their production. Also, they grieved the piece rate established by management to their union. In the first experimental condition (participation with representation), researchers found the attitudes of the workers to be the most cooperative. They worked well with the methods of the engineer and the supervisor. In the second experimental condition (total participation), the groups also worked well with their supervisor, and there was no indication of aggression observed by the researchers.

This study indicates that management can modify greatly or remove completely a group's resistance to changes in the work methods and piece rates by permitting the group to establish its own goals. Groups can push production up or down depending on the level at which the group sets them. If workers have *some* say in the changes that will immediately affect their lives, they will adjust more quickly than if these decisions come directly from an outside source of authority.

SUMMARY

All of these studies focused attention on the effects of the primary work group in industrial situations. Although their observations and methods of data collection differ, they have several findings in common. These researchers gave us further substantiation for the power and influence of work groups in organizations. They provided us with rich documentation about what can happen in the workplace if we do not address the needs, wants, and desires of the workers. The work group can be a powerful influence in getting individual workers to conform to the work behavior of others in the work group. This collective influence can be a positive force, as in the case of the aircraft studies, or it can be a restrictive force accompanied by aggression and hostility toward authority and nongroup members, as is witnessed in the Chicago studies.

The Coch and French studies are important because they proved to the practicing managers that groups can have a positive influence on worker behavior and performance. If workers are able to participate in decisions that directly affect their lives and if workers are permitted to take a large measure of control over their environment, both workers and management will profit.

Chapter Thirty-Two

Studies of Work Groups in the 1950s

We can really notice the involvement of many disciplines in the study of small group behavior in the workplace during the 1950s. The following studies offer a variety of research methodologies and theoretical bases.

ASSEMBLY-LINE STUDY

In 1952, Charles Walker and Robert H. Guest reported their study on assembly-line work and assembly-line workers. Coming from the Institute of Human Relations at Yale University, they were influenced by W. Wight Bakke. Bakke reasoned that industrial unrest lay in unidentifiable needs, wants, and wishes of the worker that were currently being denied. According to Arensberg (1951), the Bakke school is carried into the field of small groups because of the results of their analyses. They discovered that "sources of expressed satisfaction and dissatisfaction lie very close to home, oftenest in the workplace itself . . . the worker today . . . seems more concerned with . . . rewarding personal relationships with his fellow workers" (Arensberg, 1951, p. 332).

The research for *Man on the Assembly Line* began in the summer of 1949 at an automobile plant. The researchers interviewed 180 workers at their residences over a period of months in an attempt to discover information about their "life on the line." The researchers wanted to examine the following elements: (*a*) the worker's immediate job, (*b*) his relationship with his fellow workers, (*c*) pay and security, (*d*) his relationship to his supervisor, (*e*) general conditions in the plant relating to his work, (*f*) promotion and transfer, and (*g*) his relationship to the union (Walker & Guest, 1952). The researchers were also interested in seeing if the technology of the workplace would affect group formation and integration.

Workers were asked to describe their "social geography," that is, the number of men that made up their immediate work group and the amount of interaction they had with their fellow workers. Most reported that they were part of a two-to-five-man work group. Half of the men reported that they had contact with their work group every five minutes at least. Most reported that being able to talk was one of the reasons for liking their jobs, although not the principal one.

The results of the Walker and Guest study revealed that the type of work groups that formed was largely due to the requirements of the technology of the assembly line. It is also interesting to note that each member of the work group had a slightly different description of the group's composition. The perception of who belonged to what work group changed due to the assembly-line technology. The isolated workers disliked their jobs and gave social isolation as the primary cause. As Lupton (1967) pointed out, "Absenteeism and turnover were related positively to technical elements in the job such as machine pacing, repetitiveness and social deprivation" (p. 33).

Technology had an influence on work group perceptions. It affected workers' ability to interact with co-workers, and thus, it influenced whether they perceived each other as a work team. Very little of the assembly work required a team, but when it did, the members clearly expressed an awareness and identification with their fellow workers. Unfortunately, the researchers did not actually watch the process of work group formation. They did not learn to what extent the members who did not perceive themselves to be in a group or team contributed to the work-flow process or its disruption. Did they, like the bottoming room of the ABC Shoe Factory, have clues to let other workers know where they were in the assembly process? Did the work group regulate the technology at all? Did they adapt at all to their work environment? This kind of information cannot be learned from a questionnaire.

THE CASH POSTERS STUDY

George Homans presented the results of his Cash Posters Study in 1954. Homans was a sociologist, and he described his method of analysis in his book, *The Human Group*, published in 1950. He defined a group in the following manner:

> A group is a number of persons who communicate with another often over a span of time, and who are few enough so that each person is able to communicate with all others, not at secondhand, through other people, but face-to-face. Sociologists call this the primary group (p. 1).

Homans (1950) further described his mode of analysis: "What we do observe are: activities, interactions, evaluations, norms and controls" (p. 12). He believed that a group was a system evolving in an environment. Using this as his theoretical base, Homans (1954) described this study as "a case of the relations between repetitive work, individual behavior, and social organization of a clerical group" (p. 274).

From December 1949 through April 1950, Homans observed 10 women working in the clerical department in a large public utilities firm. Their job was cash posting. It was a boring and repetitive job that required no previous experience and little concentration. However, the nature of the job permitted much interaction among the women because they were moving tapes from one ledger to another.

Homans spent the first part of his time getting acquainted with the work environment and trying to gain acceptance by the workers (for he did not want to interfere with their day-to-day operations). He also wanted to get some general impressions about the behavior of the workers. He found that the group of women workers accepted him when they invited him to their Christmas party and to another party for a worker who was leaving to get married. The second stage of the study involved recording his observations of worker interaction, a sociogram of who talked with whom and how often. Every 15 minutes, Homans would scan the room and make notes about his observations. The last stage of the study was the longest because he interviewed all the women and their supervisors. This was done at the work site but in a private room. The interviews lasted from one to two hours. In order to validate his impressions, he returned to the floor for a two-week period.

Homans concluded from the observations and his interviews that 9 out of 10 women liked their job. At least five women mentioned that the friendly atmosphere was one of the positive features of the job. He also found a distinct social clique organization. It should be pointed out that there was nothing in the work itself that could account for this. An important determinant for the workers who joined together in a clique formation was where each sat at the posting table during the first year on the job. Clique members interacted with each other more than the other cash posters. The cliques also did things together both on and off the job, for example, eating lunch together or going out after work.

It is interesting to note that the one isolate in the group was also the woman most often late for work. She came from a poor side of town, did not dress well, and did not get mentioned by any of the other women as someone with whom they talked. This picture of isolation was confirmed by the sociogram. It could be that a lack of social integration and social acceptance may have been a cause for her tardiness. We also find in this study that group formation was based on similarity among group members, that is, they interacted more with those whom they perceived were like them.

One can also see Homans's theory of exchange in operation in this study. Exchange theory posits that people maximize their rewards and minimize the costs of any relationship. The members formed groups based on the degree to which they felt they were getting some reward from this formation. To become part of the group meant that they had someone to help them get through what they perceived to be a boring job. It must be pointed out, however, that the extent of their interaction did not necessarily affect positively their productivity. Most of the 10 women worked at the company standard. However, the least productive was the oldest worker and the most socially interactive.

MIDWEST MACHINE COMPANY: GROUP COHESIVENESS STUDY

Stanley Seashore reported the results of a study of Midwest Machine Company in his book, *Group Cohesiveness in the Industrial Work Group*, published in 1954. Seashore surveyed industrial workers to learn their attitudes toward a variety of subjects: the morale among employees and the interrelationship among morale, supervisory practices, and productivity. Questionnaires were administered to the employees on site in the early months of 1950. This research effort was a part of a series of studies supported by the Human Relations Program of the Survey Research Center, Institute of Social Research at the University of Michigan.

Group cohesiveness, or the degree of closeness and sense of unity, was the special focus of this research. This study advanced the following hypotheses based on the field research case studies conducted from the 1930s through the 1950s.

Hypothesis 1: Members of groups characterized by high cohesiveness will, in comparison with members of low-cohesive groups, exhibit a lowered incidence of anxiety.

Hypothesis 2: The strength of forces toward uniformity of standards within a group will be a function of the cohesiveness of the group. In the case of a group subjected to forces toward an uncertain or unobtainable goal imposed by an external agent, the point of equilibrium of forces upon the group toward and away from the goal will be a function of perceived supportiveness of the external agent.

Hypothesis 3: The degree of cohesiveness of the group is determined in part by the degree of similarity, or uniformity, among the members of the group.

Hypothesis 4: Conditions that offer increased opportunities for interaction among members of a group are positively related to the degree of group cohesiveness that is developed. (Seashore, 1954, pp. 14, 21, 24, 26)

The research population consisted of 228 section shift work groups, resulting in a total of 5,871 members. This number was arrived at through a selection process to assure that the respondents actually performed group work. The major findings of the study revealed that members of high-cohesive work groups exhibited less anxiety than did members of low-cohesive groups.

High-cohesive groups had a more effective group standard of work performance than the low-cohesive groups. High-cohesive groups also differed most from the plant performance norm in that they were either higher or lower in their production performance rate. The direction of the deviation from the production norm was a function of the degree to which the larger organization was perceived by the group as supportive. Group cohesiveness was not related to the similarity among workers regarding their age or educational backgrounds. Group cohesiveness was positively related to the group's opportunity for interaction. The more the members were able to interact with other work group members, the more cohesive they became. This points to the importance of face-to-face communication.

It should be noted that group cohesiveness was inferred from: (*a*) whether they felt part of the group; (*b*) if they wanted to stay or leave the group; or (*c*) if they felt their group was better than others. Group cohesiveness was not determined by observations of actions in the workplace.

Therefore, we do not know the extensiveness of the consequences of these group perceptions.

Seashore's research was significant in that it attempted to confirm and build on what previous researchers have told us about the behaviors of groups in the workplace. He did not use the observation techniques but rather attempted to quantify the observations of researchers that had come before him. The extensiveness of the survey form and the number of workers involved was most commendable. The use of statistical tools and correlational statistics was an attempt to confirm and shed more light on our knowledge of small groups in the work setting.

SUMMARY

The research of the 1950s marked the beginning of our break from the methodologies given to us by industrial sociologists and applied anthropologists, that is, participant observation of interactions, sentiments, and activities of the work group in its environmental setting. The research of the 1950s began the quest for quantifying what had been observed by researchers using the case study method to understand the role of groups in the workplace.

Correlational studies were presented to the readers in an attempt to explain the variables that made groups behave the way they did in the workplace. A look at the technological factors in forming these work groups was also addressed through the survey research techniques employed. The importance of the research of the 1950s is its attempt to provide us with a quantitative and comparative look at different organizational technologies in our quest to understand human group behavior in the workplace.

Chapter Thirty-Three

Studies of Work Groups in the 1960s

If the 1950s was a time for quantifying information about groups in the workplace, then the 1960s represented a time to explore any avenue of choice. This was obvious from the variety of research efforts conducted during this period of time. The following are representative of the diversity of research during this decade. It should be noted that these studies are not presented in chronological order but rather according to major schools of influence.

HARWOOD REVISITED

Harwood Manufacturing Company continued its quest to understand the problems faced by its factories and employees. In 1962, Harwood took over another pajama factory, The Weldon Company. Both Harwood and Weldon were competing in the same market, each with similar products. But one was successful and the other was not. Harwood was the successful plant, having undergone several changes in its history and having benefited from the research of Lewin, Bavelas, and Coch and French. Harwood was most anxious to transplant its organizational climate into Weldon.

In 1967, Marrow, Bowers, and Seashore explained this attempt in their book, *Management by Participation: Creating a Climate for Personal and Organizational Development*. They reported that between 1962 and 1964 an extensive change program was undertaken at the Weldon plant. Harwood served as the researchers' control group for worker performance comparison purposes.

At the beginning of the experiment, The Weldon Company had lost money, whereas Harwood Manufacturing had experienced a 17 percent profit increase during the same period of time. Something had to be done. The change program at Weldon had *five* different action-researchers during the two-year study! Some of the interventions included: engineering consultants, operator training, in-plant T-groups (training sessions) for members at senior levels, and group discussions for members at the junior levels. Something was bound to happen with all this going on, and sure enough, it did! By 1964, Weldon's profits were up 17 percent, almost up to those of Harwood, which was still ahead at 21 percent. In addition to the increase in profits achieved by the company, the operator turnover rate fell as well as the rate of absenteeism. It should be pointed out that both companies had an increase in profits during the time the study took place. This should not, however, take away from the tremendous gains of Weldon.

Harwood had already been using a participative mode of management. The researchers were aiming at this for the Weldon plant, so they adopted Likert's System 4 management model. The model posits four management styles: System 1: exploitative-authoritative; System 2: benevolent-authoritative; System 3: consultative; and System 4: participative. At the beginning of the experiment, Weldon teetered between Likert's System 1 and 2. At the end of the change program in 1964, it had shifted to System 3, the consultative management mode. Would this change in leadership style be a permanent one? In 1966, the researchers checked and found Weldon had progressed toward System 4, the participative mode of management (Smith, 1973).

What caused this shift from System 1, exploitative-authoritative, to System 4, participative? The researchers concluded that it was the "interpersonal intervention" that led to improved productivity. The climate was better. The management style was consultative and participative. Yet the technology remained basically the same except for the training interventions. Did this change in the climate of the organization foster group formation and facilitate cohesiveness among work-group members? Why didn't the workers restrict their output? Why did the workers *not* want to quit their jobs and leave the plant as other workers did in the past? The researchers did not say but one might speculate that the work group also went through changes for these results to occur. Perhaps the more pleasant interpersonal atmosphere made the workers feel part of the process. Workers developed a new identity. They liked themselves and their fellow workers. The change in supervisors' leadership style, which was now more participative, paid off. In this case, it led to an increase in production and less absenteeism.

NORWEGIAN SHOE FACTORY

In an effort to replicate the results of the Coch and French study conducted at Harwood during the 1940s, French, Israel, and Äs (1960) conducted an experiment on worker participation in a Norwegian Shoe Factory. The experiment was carried out in the assembly hall in the shoe factory. Nine four-men groups took part in this study. Four groups served as controls and five groups were assigned to various experimental groups. Two groups were permitted moderate participation in group discussions and three groups were allowed only weak participation. Their managers served as discussion leaders and were trained by the researchers in discussion techniques. It should be pointed out that the discussion group topics and decisions did not have direct relevance to the employees.

After the training intervention, questionnaire results indicated that the meetings produced "psychological participation" (French et al., 1960, p. 18). However, there was no difference between the experimental and control groups regarding their level of production. French et al. (1960) noted, "The very strong production ceilings constituted a further reason why there were no differences in production" (p. 18). They further explained that culture might also be a variable to consider regarding the differences between the American experiment and the Norwegian one. "The Norwegian workers had a stronger tradition of being organized in a union than had the workers in the American factory" (French et al., 1960, p. 18).

This study established that participation in and of itself is not a panacea for production problems. The concept of "direct relevancy" is an important one. If a group member is forced to participate in a decision-making adventure that does not have any direct bearing on the worker, the fact that the group member is participating in a group activity may not affect his or her behavior once out in the work setting. It further suggests that groups must have the appropriate legitimate power to make decisions. In this case, the power to make decisions was near zero because it was not legitimized. Therefore, the workers turned to the one force in their work life that had legitimate power and influence—the workers in their union.

As Smith (1973) pointed out, "The failure of the French et al. study relative to Coch and French serves as a timely reminder that the determinants of success or failure of such group procedures did not lie solely within the groups themselves" (p. 76).

SUMMARY OF THE GROUP PARTICIPATION STUDIES

Kurt Lewin and his three major studies with children's play groups, housewives, and finally the Harwood experiments demonstrated that the results of democratic leadership and group member involvement in decision making led to increased group productivity and membership satisfaction. Or did it? Other researchers who attempted to use Lewin's advice were less successful in achieving higher output among workers, although increased satisfaction did result. The French et al. (1960) study did point out some of the problems with the notion that participation was *the* way to achieve employee motivation.

As Bucklow (1966) explained, "Research workers such as Maier, Likert, and McGregor realized that their techniques had to be linked to the organizational framework" (p. 61). Thus, Likert used his "linking-pin theory" that stated overlapping roles should tie participation groups to all levels in the organization and Maier emphasized the importance of involving all levels of the organization in his "problem-solving" participation conferences. Maier found that group decisions should be unanimous to get the effectiveness and importance of personal worth achieved through the group. Some scholars question the relative impact of participative decision-making programs, especially if the organization does not change the distribution of rewards and the power of authority (Bucklow, 1966).

It is interesting to note that regardless of the *kind* of program one institutes to include members of the organization in decision making, unless they see the possibilities to influence, work-group norms will still govern the workers' level of productivity.

TAVISTOCK INSTITUTE

The Tavistock Human Relations Institute of London, England, actually had its beginnings in the late 1930s but it was in the 1960s that its work gained attention in the industry. A group of colleagues who worked at the Tavistock Clinic (a voluntary outpatient center for psychotherapy), in collaboration with British military administrators, conducted research during the war. They emphasized the psycho-social variables affecting the individual and the importance of the small group and its capacity to solve its own problems. They also believed that the primary group needed to be integrated with the larger organizational system (Sofer, 1972).

There were three major areas of this war-time research effort: (*a*) group selection officers; (*b*) the effects of "therapeutic communities" based on Bion's work and under his direction; and (*c*) civil resettlement work that helped military men make the transition from military life to civilian life. After the war, W. R. Bion conducted a series of group meetings for members of the Tavistock Clinic and Institute. He revealed his theory of small-group process. Sofer (1972) defined these elements as "dependence behavior, fight, flight, pairing between members, election of the 'sickest' as temporary leaders, and the emergence of 'hidden agendas'" (p. 209). Bion brought a psychoanalytic influence to the Tavistock group, but his heavy dependence on psychoanalysis and the vagueness of his group characteristics limited its use in organizations. In the 1960s, however, Bion's work was revived as a result of the development of the laboratory method of training groups in human relations. These human laboratories were similar to those developed in Bethel, Maine, at the National Training Laboratories in 1947.

In 1957, these study groups began in an effort to allow participants to examine their reactions to authority and dependence within organizations (Gorden, 1979). The focus of the activities was on the group, but through these experiences, self-awareness by the individual was inevitable. Both Elliott Jaques and I. E. P. Menzies, members of the Tavistock Institute, conducted research in the field regarding relations of group process to the structure of the social organization (Sofer, 1972). Jaques found that the problems between managers and workers arose from the managers' inability to express themselves appropriately. This difficulty in expression gave the workers a rationale for opposing management solutions or their work-performance standards.

Work groups were good at "flight" behavior. "Criticism by one group or another might serve the function of avoiding intragroup tensions" (Sofer, 1972, p. 212). Menzies found that institutions developed defensive mechanisms against tasks within the organization that led to increased anxiety. Sofer (1972) summarized the contribution of the work of Jaques and Menzies in this manner: "They expand our understanding at the same time of the psychological functions performed by persisting features of organizational life and some of the reasons why such structural features are often so intractable to change" (p. 213).

Perhaps some of the most famous studies supported by the Tavistock researchers are the coal mining studies summarized by Eric Trist and his associates in their book, *Organizational Choice*. The purpose and theoretical assumptions of these researchers are described below:

> In the present mining studies the research focus is the *socio-psychological* system. It is through the people who comprise this system that technological and economic changes are successfully or unsuccessfully implemented. For such changes to be effectively introduced, understanding of the latent as well as the manifest functioning of the socio-psychological system is necessary. (Trist, Higgin, Murray, & Pollock, 1963, p. 7)

Trist did action research in the coal mining industry in Great Britain. At that time, coal mining was an individual process. Coal miners each were skilled in the various jobs of getting coal. They selected their own work groups. Even though they worked by themselves, they were paid according to how much coal their group was able to mine. Thus, the group shared equally the fruits of their individual labor. This created an atmosphere that was harmonious because they were not competing with one another for their salaries.

With the introduction of the "long wall" method of coal mining, the workers had to specialize. Their jobs no longer were able to be accomplished alone. Each work shift had a specific function to perform to complete the coal mining process. The long wall method did not prove to be very successful. The members of each shift were unable to work together as before in a harmonious way. In addition, it meant that they were dependent on other work groups to get the job done. Long wall mining required coordination among the various work shifts. The work group no longer was autonomous as it had been using the conventional coal mining method. They were no longer able to control their work environment; they had to depend on other shifts and other bosses for the work to get done.

Trist helped restructure the work group's jobs bringing back their autonomy despite mining's changing technology. Consequently, there was no sharp division of labor between the work shifts as in the conventional long wall method. As Lupton (1966) pointed out, "The team as a whole is given and accepts responsibility for the deployment of men to shifts and jobs" (p. 46). Tavistock concepts thus returned the mining work group to the traditional values favored by the workers. Once again, they had control over their fate.

Bucklow (1966) summarized the contribution of the Tavistock coal mining studies in this manner:

> It has been argued that the Tavistock concept of the autonomous work group goes far towards solving some of the problems of worker motivation, participation, and

power equalization, with which American researchers are preoccupied. The Tavistock concept also provides a new role for the work group different from that advocated by Mayo, Lewin and Likert. (p. 74)

In his studies of the Indian Textile Mills, Rice confirmed the importance of autonomous work groups. Rice viewed the organization as a series of "encapsulated significant environments" (Lupton, 1966, p. 87). The work-group environment was very important. According to Rice, the primary task of organizations was to shape the structure of work groups in such a way that allows them to perform their jobs in as efficient a manner as possible, that is, to adapt to the internal and external forces of the work environment.

NATIONAL TRAINING LABORATORIES: T-GROUPS

Kurt Lewin had a major influence in the development of the training laboratory method in the United States. The National Training Laboratory (NTL) in Bethel, Maine, started in 1947 (Gorden, 1979). The training groups, or T-groups as they were called, were designed to allow participants to experience the dynamics of the small-group process and their reaction to it. In 1957 and 1958, however, a new training program was introduced to the members of the NTL. According to Bucklow (1966), "The most important was that conducted by the Employee Relations Department of the Esso Company under the leadership of R. R. Blake, J. S. Mouton, and H. A. Shepard from the Southwest Human Relations Laboratory of the University of Texas" (p. 63).

Robert Blake and Jane Mouton (1964) later adapted the T-group to a more structured approach to training that they called the Managerial Grid®. The Grid was designed to help managers and groups assess their managerial styles and attitudes toward the worker and work. The two dimensions of the Grid are: (a) a concern for people and (b) a concern for production. Depending on one's answers to a questionnaire, one could plot behavior on the Grid. For example, the most effective manager and group would be high on both concern for people and concern for production (i.e., a 9.9 on the Grid).

Chris Argyris also was influenced by the National Training Laboratory method. He was a proponent of the T-group method, although he realized some of its weaknesses. He asserted that one of the barriers to managerial decision-making effectiveness was an inability on the part of managers to trust workers, to *own* their own feelings, and to accept others by being open minded. In 1966, Argyris reported the results in the *Harvard Business Review* of his analysis on the behavior of 165 top executives derived from six companies. He looked at two major categories of behaviors: (a) how often the executives owned up to and accepted responsibility for their ideas and feelings or failed to do so, how often they opened up to others' ideas, or how they helped others to open up and the degree of risk they took when presenting their ideas or feelings; and (b) the norms of the executive culture, both positive and negative. In addition to this analysis of executive behavior in meetings, he also observed the men at work and conducted taped interviews.

The results of his analysis revealed the executives rarely exhibited high-quality interpersonal behaviors in the decision-making meetings. They rarely took risks, rarely helped others own up to their ideas or feelings, rarely supported and trusted others, and rarely expressed their feelings. Argyris (1966) warned against the consequences of such behavior. He concluded that when individuals feel that their expressions of ideas and feelings are not valued, they may "build personal and organizational defenses to help them suppress their own feelings or inhibit others in such expression" (p. 87). This lack of expressiveness may result in less commitment to decisions. That is, individuals will fake support because dissent is not an accepted norm of behavior. This might also result in what Argyris termed "gamesmanship."

Still another consequence is a lack of awareness. Executives thought that a lack of disagreement during the decision-making meetings meant that everyone agreed with the discussions, got along, and trusted each other. The executives were totally unaware of the negative feelings their subordinates had about them.

Argyris (1966) further suggested several ways of overcoming these interpersonal barriers. One useful technique he used was to have the groups tape their meetings and then play back the tapes. With the help of Argyris, they were able to analyze their behaviors, and find ways to improve them. T-groups were another suggested alternative. He believed that these types of outside programs were a good way for managers to become aware of their behaviors. However, one drawback was that the whole organization could not go through the program—just one or two executives, thus, the "biggest payoff is for the individual" (Argyris, 1966, p. 97).

In his book, *Organization and Innovation,* Argyris (1965) presented 10 signs of group interpersonal competence. (You may recall that these signs were first introduced in Chapter 2 and again in Chapter 13.) He suggested that these signs could be used to determine the group's "teamness" or developing group teamness:

1. Contributions made with the group are additive.
2. The group moves forward as a unit; there is a sense of team spirit; high involvement.
3. Decisions are made by consensus.
4. Commitment to decisions by most members is strong.
5. The group continually evaluates itself.
6. The group is clear about its goals.
7. Conflict is brought out into the open and dealt with.
8. Alternative ways of thinking about solutions are generated.
9. Leadership tends to go to the individual best qualified.
10. Feelings are dealt with openly. (p. 264)

SUMMARY

The research of the 1960s, like the political and social climate of that time, represented a revolution of ideas and the breaking of traditions. The research studies offered us a "new way" of exploring the behavior of the work group not just through observational techniques or recording and measuring instruments but through planned change: change and adaptation to the social technology of the work environment as in the Tavistock coal studies and changes in the managerial climate as in the Harwood study. The Tavistock study group and the National Training Laboratory's common emphasis on self-learning and self-awareness of one's behavior in the small-group setting became an important tool for redirecting and changing perceptions of the work environment and the worker.

The 1930s through the 1950s research laid the foundation for the research of the 1960s in understanding the effects of groups in the workplace. It was now time to do something about this knowledge and provide managers with the tools to become more effective and responsive to their workers and their work environment by helping them learn a new method of dealing with the work group. Creating a work climate that presented not only a concern for production, but also a concern for people, was of utmost importance. A manager who listened to subordinates, trusted them, and was open and encouraged openness in the most participative way, were all characteristics leading to effective teamwork.

Are these ideas really revolutionary? Not really, but it was in the 1960s that they soared in importance.

Chapter Thirty-Four

Work Group Action Research in More Recent Times

Research during the last three decades has centered on helping organizations deal with the ever-advancing problems brought about from a global economy. Worker strikes, absenteeism, productivity and quality control problems, lockouts, employee buyouts, cooperatives, and foreign competition have all led to a different work environment. Most of the scholarly work conducted during this period has centered on case studies of companies that succeeded while dealing with some kind of adversity. We will be exploring three such movements in this chapter: (*a*) the quality circle/total quality management movement; (*b*) the socio-technical experiments in Scandinavian countries and the U.S. Saturn experience; and (*c*) employee ownership programs.

QUALITY CIRCLES AND TOTAL QUALITY MANAGEMENT MOVEMENT

Sundstrom, De Meuse, and Futrell (1990) defined work teams as "interdependent collections of individuals who share responsibility for specific outcomes for their organizations" (p. 120). They further classified four work-team applications: (*a*) advice and involvement, including quality circles and employee involvement groups; (*b*) production and service groups, such as autonomous self-regulating groups; (*c*) projects and development, or white collar quality circles; and (*d*) action and negotiation groups. Perhaps there is no single organizational intervention that has received more publicity and more popularity than *quality control circles* or *quality circles*.

Two Americans, W. Edwards Deming and Joseph M. Juran, are credited with bringing the ideas of employee participation and quality control to Japan after World War II. After the war, the words "Made in Japan" were equivalent to saying "cheap, inferior products." These beliefs had to be reversed, and so the Japanese set out to change their image and to enhance the quality of the products they produced for exporting.

Professor Deming was invited to Japan by General MacArthur after World War II. It was there that Deming taught the Japanese the concepts of statistical quality control (SQC) and total quality control. "During the 1950s and the 1960s, the Japanese Union of Scientists and Engineers (JUSE) and the Japanese government widely disseminated the idea of quality control through publications along with radio and television series" (Wood, Hull, & Azumi, 1983).

In 1961 Kaoru Ishikawa, an engineering professor at Tokyo University, suggested that small groups of workers be formed to address problems in their respective work areas. He began by conducting workshop discussion groups using quality control statistical techniques as problem-solving mechanisms. Ishikawa drew on the work of Likert, Argyris, McGregor, and Herzberg, whose writings were already well known in Japan. Early work groups focused primarily on quality, and these groups eventually became known as quality control circles. Quality circles (QCs) are primarily problem-solving groups. The work-group members apply problem-solving methods and group processes to production or work problems. The first quality circle conference was held in Japan in May 1963. Thus, the origins of *quality circles, quality control circles, employee-participation circles,* or *employee-communications circles* in the United States; *work councils* in Sweden; *jishu kanri, ringi,* or *newawashi* in Japan; and *samaeul* in Korea began.

In 1974, the concept of quality circles found its way to the United States. Lockheed's space and missile unit in Sunnyvale, California, adopted the Japanese version of quality circles. It became the managerial fad of the 1980s. One reason for the rapid rise of quality-circle groups is best explained by examining the labor situation during that time.

Secretary of Labor James Donovan, when characterizing the United States' lack of productivity and its steady decline since the mid 1960s, remarked: "We are no longer talking about a slow-down in productivity growth, we are now experiencing an extended period of absolute decline in our production efficiency" (Mohr & Mohr, 1983, p. 4). Something had to be done quickly, and the success of Japanese quality control circles became not only intriguing, but promising.

Early proponents of QCs turned to this employee participation technique hoping to improve quality, improve communications, increase productivity, reduce the adversarial position between union and management, to deal with an alienated, overeducated workforce, to offset foreign competition, and, some also hoped, to lessen the influence of unions in the workplace (Kornbluh, 1984; Lawler, Mohrman, & Ledford, 1992; Wolfe, Hauck, & Varny, 1984). According to Wood et al. (1983):

> Three of the Lockheed managers involved left the company and became active as consultants, these three managers developed a wide array of education and training materials that define the standard contents and processes for most American QC programs. In 1978, the former Lockheed managers founded the International Association of Quality Circles (IAQC) to provide an institutionalized forum for discussing and promoting the QC idea. (p. 39)

Proponents of QCs claimed lower absenteeism and turnover rate, increases in productivity and work satisfaction, and savings of millions of dollars in production costs as the benefits for instituting QCs in an organization. Steel and Lloyd (1988) could find only marginal support for the efficacy of QCs, however. They found that QC participation had a positive influence on cognitive measures of competence and interpersonal trust, and decreases in employee withdrawal.

Even Juran questioned the viability of implementing in the United States quality circles that were so successful in Japan. "The Japanese sense of organizational loyalty and work group solidarity tends to considerably ease the implementation of QCs in Japan. Work group peer pressure to participate is very strong in Japan" (Wolfe et al., 1984). Interestingly, Wood et al.'s (1983) analysis of 50 Japanese factories found that the best predictors for increased productivity and improved morale were a larger market share and mass production techniques, not necessarily the use of quality circles. In fact, most of the evidence supporting the use of quality circles comes from self-reported success stories or case studies. "For all the interest in and adoption of QCs in the U.S., it is ironic that this goes on in spite of a lack of reliable evidence that QCs are effective either here or in Japan" (Wood et al., 1983, p. 49).

The QC movement has evolved into a great emphasis on teamwork. Sometimes that entails employee involvement, self-directed work groups, natural work groups, workouts, and semi-autonomous work groups. Lawler et al. (1992) reported that 77 percent of the 313 *Fortune* 1,000 companies they surveyed had total quality management programs. Of these, 17 percent said they had all employees covered by a total quality program. Quality circles were used in more than 66 percent of the *Fortune* 1,000 companies; however, most of the programs involved less than one-fifth of the organization's workers. There was a 16 percent increase from 1987 to 1990 in the use of other employee problem solving groups or teams, and a small increase in the union and management quality of work life (QWL) committees.

Although quality circles or employee involvement programs and total quality management programs may be in operation at one organization, they do differ from one another. Total quality management programs may establish different kinds of employee participation. Their emphasis is on developing self-managing, problem-solving teams rather than depending on inspectors to do quality control. Total quality management programs often cut across organizational lines through direct employee involvement. They require that all employees participate in the quality enhancement program. Total quality management implementation tends to be more top-down and more management initiated and controlled. Quality circles work more at the bottom of the organization (Lawler et al., 1992).

According to Mohr and Mohr (1983), there are 10 fundamental characteristics for quality control activities:

1. Self-development.
2. Volunteerism.
3. Group activities.
4. Participation by all.
5. Use of quality circle techniques.
6. Activities closely related to the workshop.
7. Enhancing and continuing quality circle activities.
8. Mutual development.
9. Creativity.
10. Quality consciousness (p. 14).

In addition, quality circle techniques include such tools as brainstorming, cause-effect diagrams, Pareto diagrams, histograms, checksheets, case studies, graphs, scatter diagrams, sampling, and data collection and analysis. These seem like activities that should be effective and helpful. Why, then, do quality circles or employee-involvement programs frequently fail?

One explanation might be in the misassumption that workers actually desire participation and that minor participation is workplace democracy. Some American workers actually resent the quasi participation of some workteam programs. As Ferris and Wagner (1985) pointed out, "QCs management does not provide workers with actual control, but merely with the 'illusion of control' by offering them the chance to provide input that the organization subsequently ignores" (p. 159). If the organizational decision-making culture is such that "only the people at the top make the decisions around here," implementing QC or QWL problem-solving groups will be futile and frustrating for the workers, causing more harm than good.

In 1988, Stohl and Jennings explored the role of employee voice and volunteerism on quality circles. They contended that many quality circles rely on workers who volunteer to participate in the programs. As they pointed out, volunteerism eliminates the disinterested, the hostile, and the uncooperative. But why do workers volunteer to participate? One explanation offered by Stohl and Jennings (1988) is that this is one way that employees can voice their dissatisfaction or express their concerns on issues that affect them in the workplace. Workers have three basic means of expressing their dissatisfaction. They can: (*a*) exit or leave the organization, (*b*) remain loyal and suffer in silence, or (c) voice their concerns. Voicing dissatisfaction depends on the communicative ability of the worker, the cost perceived of voicing his/her concern, and support from the worker or work group.

In their study of volunteers and nonvolunteers of an organization's QCs, Stohl and Jennings found that volunteers and nonvolunteers both expressed loyalty to the company. Volunteers of QCs were dissatisfied with parts of their jobs and joined the group in hopes of making their work life better. Volunteers also saw the QCs as a means of expressing themselves to someone. Prior to their joining the QCs, workers expressed a sense of frustration with not being able to talk about their dissatisfaction with aspects of their work. However, Stohl and Jennings also found that volunteering for QCs increases workers' expectations that something will improve. In fact, volunteers were less satisfied than those who did not volunteer. This can have far-reaching consequences. Research has demonstrated that workers who leave QCs are often significantly more negative and dissatisfied than they were prior to joining the circles. This negative experience makes them more resistant to future management interventions.

There are several conditions, however, where quality circles and employee participation programs can survive. Drago (1988) found three conditions that can account for quality-circle survival in organizations. Quality circles survive when:

- There is greater worker participation in managerial decisions.
- There is a fear of job loss.
- The workers are relatively unskilled. (p. 349)

Buller and Bell (1986) concluded that "individual performance is a function of an individual's ability, motivation, effort, and strategies for performance—all moderated by the nature of the task being performed. To the extent that immediate work groups enhance or hinder these mechanisms, they enhance or hinder performance" (p. 307).

SOCIO-TECHNICAL EXPERIMENTS OF THE SCANDINAVIAN COUNTRIES

The application of the socio-technical concepts derived from the Tavistock Institute came to fruition in the quality of work-life action research in Sweden. The Swedish model is grounded in equality or egalitarian principles and values held in such high esteem in the Swedish culture. The Saltsjöbaden Agreement of 1938 mandated a spirit of cooperation between labor and management: "Employers and employees shall cooperate to establish a good working environment" (Söderlund, 1987, p. 6). This was echoed in the Security of Employment Act (1974, 1984), the 1978 Work Environment Act, and later in the mid-1980s with the Swedish Leadership Organization and Codetermination Program (LOM). LOM encouraged a democratic dialogue and development of communication competence in the workplace (Gorden, Holmberg, & Heisey, 1994). According to Gorden et al. (1994), the "theory of the LOM program was that codetermination is not simply a matter of representatives of employers and unions to negotiate. If it is to be real, all parties must have a vital *say* in work matters. Reticence must be overcome in democratic dialogue" (p. 9).

Research during the 1970s tested the assumption that implementing autonomous work groups would yield increased job satisfaction leading to lower absenteeism and turnover rates. In fact, there is little empirical evidence to support this conclusion except for some case study analyses. The work group does play an important role in all aspects of the work environment in many companies in Sweden; however, the extensive use of the work group and the groups' degree of autonomy varies greatly throughout and within organizations. In fact, not all work group members develop the levels of competency or the flexibility needed to have effective work group productivity that was hoped for in the LOM program. Additionally, fluctuation of work group membership can also be harmful to the productivity and morale of the work team. Despite all this, there is an advantage to the work team concept. That is, not all members must possess high levels of work qualifications to have a successful work team because, again, none of us is as smart as all of us. An examination of the Volvo experiments to "reprofessionalize the auto worker" through integrative work teams may prove insightful.

Volvo was the company at which experiments in semi-autonomous work groups took the place of Taylorism assembly-line work with its strict division of labor and centralized organizational hierarchy. Auer and Riegler (1990) suggested that Volvo "has been seen as a forerunner in innovations in work organization since the 1970s" (p. 10).

The Kalmar Plant on the Baltic Sea was the site for a new revolutionary assembly line technique using small work groups. The organizational structure was much flatter than in the typical assembly-line organization with its layers of supervisors. This resulted in fewer white collar workers. The socio-technical concepts of the Tavistock Institute came to reality at this plant not only through the reorganization or humanization of the work force by using work teams plantwide, but also in the architecture of the plant that permitted small separate workshops for the work groups, including separate entrances to the work setting. Within the work groups, jobs were rotated, individual feedback systems were instituted, "first time right" quality control was followed, and each group developed its own hierarchy (Auer & Riegler, 1990).

The leaders of the work group emerged naturally and usually were the older, more skilled workers. These group leaders would be responsible for training new workers and would take on the role traditionally held by the supervisors. Even so, the foreman was responsible for work group productivity and production results of two work groups. There was one quality inspector for every two teams, and generally there was one supervisor for every 68 subordinates.

In the end, the humanization of the workplace achieved mixed results. One positive result was the superior production performance of the Kalmar plant when compared with other Volvo plants. For example, it took fewer worker hours to produce a car. However, the humanization of the workplace did not receive the anticipated and hoped for results. As Auer and Riegler (1990) reported, "the initial euphoria in some circles quickly gave way to disillusionment" (p. 26). In fact, this change in technology led to fewer break times, increases in the speed of production, and no real job enrichment for the workers. In actuality, work was not changed much for the benefit of the Volvo worker.

Even in this progressive work environment, employees reported an expressed need to have more "voice" in job design, production goals, and the organization of work groups. Results from a survey of 39 production workers reinforced this view. Workers reported they had little or no involvement in the decision on how to do their work. Eighty percent felt they had no influence on the speed of work, and another 80 percent said they had no opportunity to acquire additional knowledge and skills for their work, although they would have liked to see it happen and it was one of the goals of the program (Auer & Riegler, 1990). The results of these innovations repeated themselves in other experiments attempting a socio-technical marriage at Torslanda TUN plant, Torslanda TC plant, Uddevalla, and Skövde.

Given these findings, Auer and Riegler (1990) concluded, "Volvo is one of the few companies where management, employees and trade unions have found broad opportunities for gathering experience in changing the organization of work and that the company is a place of learning of organizational change" (p. 52).

From these experiments we can conclude that the success of the autonomous work group is dependent on several factors. Work groups can be effective if:

- The labor force is accustomed to working independently.
- The labor force is skilled.
- Values of autonomy, hard work, and punctuality are accepted by the work force.
- The plant is new (green field) as compared to an old factory being restructured.
- The hierarchy is flatter (decentralized) and this type of worker relationship is accepted by organizational members.
- Job rotation and enrichment is used when work groups have low level skills.
- Job enrichment, decentralized production of responsibility, and humanization principles are used for highly automated work.
- Decision-making power is granted to the work group regarding job design, production, and skill development.

THE UNITED STATES SATURN EXPERIENCE

The U.S. counterpart to the marriage of the labor union and management groups is the Saturn Corporation. Saturn, located in Spring Hill, Tennessee, is a separate subsidiary of the General Motors Corporation and is not financially dependent on it. Saturn's joint labor–management groups have been involved at all levels of the decision-making process including retailing, sales, marketing, and product process design. "Its intent was for the union to be a full partner in decision making through consensus at all levels of the organization with the right to block decisions and provide alternatives based on needs of the people and the business" (Rubinstein, Bennett, & Kochan, 1993, p. 342). There are four major joint decision-making groups present at the Saturn Corporation:

1. Decision rings—joint labor–management off-line committees.
2. Work units—self directed on-line work teams.
3. Problem resolution circles—off-line problem-solving groups.
4. Partnering—the one-on-one interaction program resulting in co-management between union, management, and workers.

Saturn also assures that workers have the skills necessary to participate in these work teams. Each new Saturn employee receives from 350 to 700 hours of training before being permitted to build a car. The work force is trained in work-team organization, problem solving, decision making, conflict resolution, and labor history. They are also trained in areas "traditionally reserved for management including budgeting, business planning and scheduling, cost analysis, manufacturing methods, ergonomics, industrial engineering, job design, accounting, record keeping, statistical process control, design of experiments and data analyses" (Rubinstein et al., 1993, p. 350).

It is too early to assess the long-range results of the Saturn experience. If Saturn can learn from past innovative organizations, it just might avoid the pitfalls that plagued other worker–management quality-of-work-life programs.

EMPLOYEE OWNERSHIP PROGRAMS

In 1977 when the workers at the Sheet and Tube Campbell Works steel company in Youngstown, Ohio, attempted an employee buyout, neither the public nor the workers were quite ready to accept the fact that employees can actually own and run a company successfully. Since that time, employee ownership has been the acceptable alternative to plant closings or takeovers.

According to Bell (1988), there are three types of employee ownership programs:

1. Conventional corporations—all or most employees own stock, and no one but employees owns stock in the company.
2. Cooperatives—democratically based organizations stressing one vote per member with all members having the right to work and a return in the profits.
3. Employee stock ownership plans (ESOP)—an attempt to decentralize plant ownership by granting employees opportunities to buy stock in the company.

These employee owned/involved organizations usually arise out of traditional organizational work life in an effort to avoid a plant closing or shutdown, a hostile takeover, or to save jobs. Due to new tax breaks and governmental financial support for ESOPs, ESOPS have become the most advantageous and thus the most popular of the three programs.

For employee-owned organizations to be effective, the employees must undergo intensive training in democratic processes (Gorden, 1994). "Without employee participation in the decisions made at shopfloor, department, and company levels, the benefits of worker ownership can be more apparent than real" (Logue, Quilligan, & Weissman, 1985, p. 18). However, decisions in these organizations are often arrived at through group consensus in an attempt to please all parties. According to Harrison (1994), "interaction in group meetings can be long, arduous, and sometimes fraught with conflict" (p. 264).

Studies have demonstrated that employee ownership alone does not necessarily mean increased productivity. What would improve productivity, researchers conclude, is a strong training system and a rich democratic communication environment coupled with ownership.

Employee stock ownership plans can be beneficial to small businesses with owners near retirement. Of 65 small businesses instituting employee ownership plans surveyed by Cohen and Quarrey, none failed when the employer retired (Bell, 1988).

In their study of Ohio-based employee-owned businesses, Logue et al. (1985) distinguished successful companies from their failed counterparts. Successful employee-owned companies:

- Used substantial public and private funds available in a timely manner.
- Began with a stable, experienced workforce.
- Had shared commitment from production workers and managers.
- Had relevant and timely information regarding the buyout.
- Maintained democratic and participatory atmosphere with equal distribution and control over the work environment.

EPILOGUE

What have we learned from our legacy of work groups? The research from the 1920s through the 1990s provides researchers of organizational small group behavior with a rich legacy of the effects of small groups in the workplace. We know that whether they are recognized or sanctioned by the organization, groups form in the workplace for any number of reasons. Their formation results from the task, the technology of the organization, the organizational climate or work environment, and the personality of members. Once groups form, they develop a structure and normative standards to perpetuate their existence. This might be done through activities both on and off the job, through their interaction with others or lack of interaction, through symbolic games, or through whatever activities will assure that group members adhere to the group's norms. What we have learned from our legacy of group research in the workplace is summarized below.

Groups in the workplace form for a variety of reasons with or without the sanctions of management.

- Groups in the workplace have a facilitating effect on jobs that are perceived to be boring and do not require concentration.
- Stress may draw members together and add to their cohesiveness.
- Groups may form because of a common fate or goal.
- Groups will pull together in response to felt inequities in the pay system or in the division of labor.
- Groups may form in response to an autocratic managerial style.
- Groups may form to satisfy the worker's need for affiliation with others.
- Groups may form as a means of aiding the workers' identification with others and to aid their assimilation into the workplace environment.
- A lack of group assimilation may result in absenteeism, tardiness, and turnover.
- Groups may form or not form because of the technological structure of the work (i.e., assembly line, coal mining, cash posting).
- Groups may form to have more control over their work environment.

Group formation in the workplace can have a variety of effects.

- Through social control, groups can increase or decrease production output.
- Interaction is often the result of group formation, but increases in worker interaction do not necessarily result in increased productivity.
- Groups conform to the group standards or norms to the extent that the group attitudes, beliefs, and values are consistent with or can be adapted to the individual's belief and value systems.
- If groups are formed as a result of felt inequities, restriction in group output may occur.
- Cohesiveness of group members increases the members' satisfaction, but may not result in increased productivity.
- One result of group formation is increased power and control.
- Social compliance is another result of group formation, and the group develops constraints to see that members follow the established rules.

What we have learned about the effects of groups in the workplace? Groups are important to organizations. They are the organization! With an understanding of why groups form in the workplace and the results of such formation, managers can facilitate the positive aspects of group formation and behavior, thus avoiding the negative impact of the work group.

We know that many factors come into play when examining groups in the workplace: organizational structure, style of leadership and the resultant attitudes toward the workers, technology, spatial ecology, and the amount of group identification or similarity among workers. All of these factors can influence in some way the effects of groups in the workplace.

It is important that we remember the lessons from the past. Participation without legitimate power and influence is neither effective nor worthwhile.

This was obvious when we examined quality circles, problem-solving teams, quality of work life, and total quality management programs. If work groups have little say in the decisions that affect their lives, they will have little ownership in them. If the corporate atmosphere is not one of trust and openness, there is little chance for high worker commitment. If we have only a few workers participate in programs such as this, we may be creating an in-group clique or an elitist group that may antagonize other work members.

Research from the past can tell us much about how we should guide our groups in the workplace—lest we forget.

APPENDIXES

Appendix A

"Work at Work" and "Roll with Roles" Notecards

Each of the following roles should be placed on a 4" x 6" notecard. Divide the notecards by the number of participants.

Role 1—Energizer: Your task is to prod the other group members into action.

Role 2—Comedian: Your task is to interject humor into the group situation.

Role 3—Dominator: Your task is to monopolize group time by presenting long, drawn out monologues.

Role 4—Initiator: Your task is define the problem, propose solutions, and offer ideas.

Role 5—Encourager: Your task is to provide support, praise, and acceptance of those who offer any type of verbal expression.

Role 6—Special-interest pleader: Your task is to periodically bring up irrelevant information and support it.

Role 7—Information seeker: Your task is to ask for clarification and solicit information from others.

Role 8—Harmonizer: Your task is to be aware of potential conflict and reduce any tension that arises between members.

Role 9—Aggressor: Your task is to attack other group members in order to protect your own status.

Role 10—Orienter: Your task is to keep the group on track with the discussion.

Role 11—*Gatekeeper:* Your task is to regulate the evenness of participation.

Role 12—Deserter: Your task is to withdraw from the group discussion.

Role 13—Secretary: Your task is to keep a written record of the group's proceedings. Make sure that you volunteer for this role!

Role 14—Follower: Your task is to go along with everyone else.

Role 15—Blocker: Your task is to interfere with the group process by making negative comments about the other group members.

Appendix B

"Work at Work" and "Roll with Roles" Sheet

Task Roles:

initiator
information seeker
energizer
orienter
secretary

Relationship Roles:

encourager
harmonizer
comedian
gatekeeper
follower

Self-Interest Roles:

blocker
aggressor
dominator
deserter
special-interest pleader

Appendix C

"Piecing It Together"
Gameboard and Puzzle Pieces

Gameboard

The gameboard is prepared in advance as diagrammed. Players cut out their appropriate tab to fit into those shapes in the management perimeter. They then negotiate with adjacent pieces to either cut their tab or cut into their piece to construct a close fit.

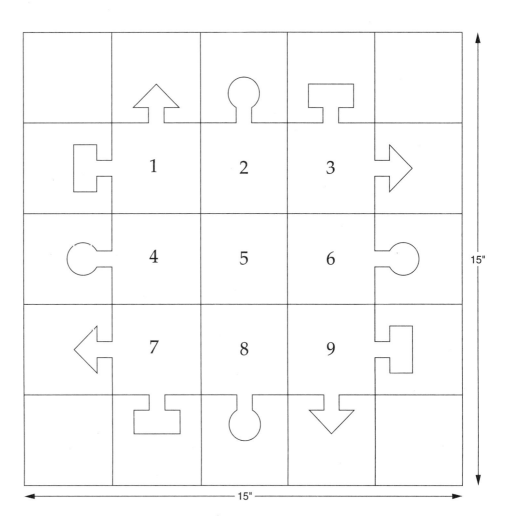

Puzzle Pieces   You will need 9 pieces. Each piece should have a different number (i.e., 1 to 9). Each piece is 3″ by 3″ with 1″ tabs.

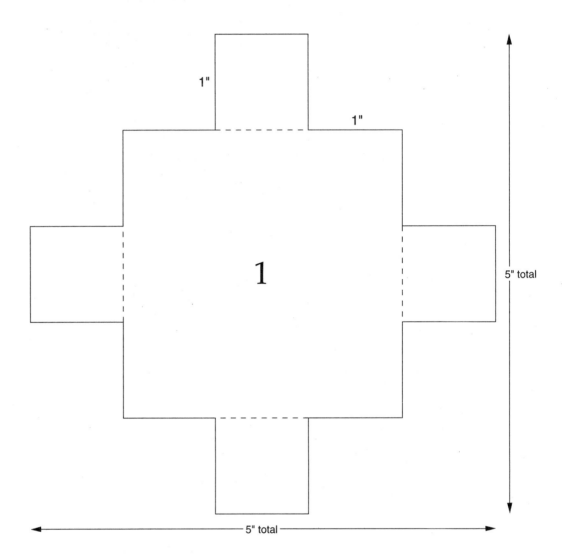

Appendix D

"Listen and You Will Hear" Script

George Jones works in an auto plant and makes $18 an hour on regular days and double-time on holidays.

On the fourth Monday in May, George's wife called and told him that their drains were plugged and water was overflowing into nearly every room in the house. He immediately told his boss that there was an emergency at home and that he would have to use one of his personal days to take care of the problem. The boss agreed and George left for home.

On his way home, George stopped at the rental center and picked up a roto-rooter machine, which rented for a full day at the flat rate of $45.

An hour after George left from work, his son was helping him lift the machine out of his car. It took the two of them nearly two hours to clear the drain lines and another two hours to clean up the mess and return the machine.

Despite the hassles and all of the yelling that had to be done, George was quite proud of himself. If he had called a plumber, the job would have cost around $100.

Questions:
1. How much money does George make an hour?
2. How many hours of work did George miss?
3. How many hours did it take him to get the job done himself?
4. How much money did George save by doing the job himself?

Solutions:
1. Ordinarily, George makes $18 an hour. However, the fourth Monday in May is a legal holiday (Memorial Day). George would have been making $36 per hour on this day.
2. George missed approximately seven hours of an eight-hour shift.
3. From the time George left the plant until he returned from the rental center approximately five hours had elapsed.
4. At his regular pay rate (7 hours X $18 = $126) plus the $45 for the machine ($126 + $45) = $171, George lost $71. Unfortunately, this was a double-time day. George lost even more [(7 hours X $36) + ($45 - $100)] = $197.

Appendix E

"The Role of Roles" Notecards

Each of the following roles should be placed on a 4" x 6" notecard.

Role 1—Task leader: Your task is to lead the group discussion by showing the others that you have a firm grasp of the discussion topic. You need to speak often and clearly. Above anything else, you must relay to the group that you want to do things fairly and democratically.

Role 2—Cheerleader: Your task is to be aware of the "emotional heartbeat" of the group. You are responsible for each individual member's satisfaction with the group. Speak to the group members about the group assignment and about their personal lives. Above anything else, you are to be sincere, nice, empathic, and sensitive to the needs of all group members.

Role 3—Tension releaser: Your task is to provide humor for the group. You must recognize when humor is needed and welcomed. You are not to be the group clown per se, but you need to insert humor where it can be appreciated. Above anything else, you must be productive while being humorous. The humor should be facilitative, not debilitative.

Role 4—Information provider: Your task is to provide the information that is necessary for the group to make a decision. In this case, you may need to improvise or make up information, but the key here is to supply the group with details, suggestions, statistics, etc. However, in real work situations information should never be fabricated. Information should be factual. Offer to take notes for the group. Above anything else, you are to supplement any suggestions made by the group with information.

Role 5—Devil's advocate: Your task is to challenge the others in the group by asking questions and offering criticism. You are not to be nasty to the other group members, but you are expected to force the group to rethink any decision or suggestion. Above anything else, you are playing the devil's advocate. Focus on the message, not the messenger.

Appendix F

"Do Not Cross" Notecards

Each of the following words should be placed on a separate 4" x 6" notecard.

manager
receptionist
student intern
vice president
president
executive secretary
worker
student intern
worker
worker

Appendix G

"A Smile or a Frown?" Notecards

Each of the following statements and emotions should be placed on a separate 4" x 6" notecard.

Set 1

I am fine.
What a lovely day.
Life is grand.
What a week.
I cannot wait until summer.
I needed that.
I believe you.
She surprised me.
He will be angry when he finds out.
I love Monday morning.

Set 2

Anger
Fear
Disgust
Contempt
Surprise
Happiness
Sadness
Interest
Determination
Bewilderment

Resources

CHAPTER 1

Case, J. (1993, September). What the experts forgot to mention. *INC.*, 68–78.

Derry, R. (1991). Institutionalizing ethical motivation: Reflections on goodplaster's agenda. In R. E. Freeman (Ed.), *Business ethics: The state of the art* (pp. 121–136). New York: Oxford Press.

Dumaine, B. (1990, May 7). Who needs a boss? *Fortune*, 52–60.

Dyer, W.G. (1977). *Team building: Issues and alternatives*. Reading, MA: Addison-Wesley.

Dygert, C.B. (1993). *Success is a team effort*. Columbus, OH: Motivational Enterprises.

Gorden, W.I., & Howe, R.J. (1977). *Team dynamics in developing organizations*. Dubuque, IA: Kendall/Hunt.

Hoerr, J. (1989, July 10). The payoff from teamwork. *Business Week*, 56–62.

Jackall, R. (1988). *Moral mazes: The world of corporate managers*. New York: Oxford University Press.

Jacob, R. (1992, May 18). The search for the organization of tomorrow. *Fortune*, 91–98.

Katzenbach, J.R., & Smith, D.K. (1993, March/April). The discipline of teams. *Harvard Business Review*, 111–120.

Katzenbach, J. R., & Smith, D.K. (1993). *The wisdom of teams: Creating the high-performance organization*. Cambridge, MA: Harvard University Press.

Ketchum, L.D., & Trist, E. (1992). *All teams are not created equal*. Thousand Oaks, CA: Sage.

Larson, C.E., & Lafasto, F.M. (1989). *Teamwork: What must go right/what can go wrong*. Thousand Oaks, CA: Sage.

Neumeier, S. (1992, March 9). Companies to watch. *Fortune*, 63.

Woodruff, D., Treece, J.B., Bhragara, S.W., & Miller, K.L. (1992, August 17). Saturn: GM finally has a real winner. But success is bringing a fresh batch of problems. *Business Week*, 88–91.

CHAPTER 2

Argyris, C. (1965). *Organization and innovation*. Homewood, IL: Richard D. Irwin.

Blake, R., & Mouton, J. (1964). *The managerial grid*. Houston, TX: Gulf.

Dyer, W.G. (1977). *Team building: Issues and alternatives*. Reading, MA: Addison-Wesley.

Gorden, W.I., & Howe, R.J. (1977). *Team dynamics in developing organizations*. Dubuque, IA: Kendall/Hunt.

Gorden, W.I., & Nevins, R.J. (1993). *We mean business: Building communication competence in business and professions*. New York: Harper Collins.

Kanter, R.M. (1983). *The change masters*. New York: Simon and Schuster.

Likert, R. (1961). *New patterns of management*. New York: McGraw-Hill.

Mayo, E. (1933). *The human problems of an industrial civilization*. Boston: Harvard University Press.

McGregor, D. (1960). *The human side of enterprise*. New York: McGraw-Hill.

Waterman, R. (1987). *The renewal factor*. New York: Bantam.

CHAPTER 3

Glines, D. (1987). What's new at the zoo? *The Quality Circle Journal, 10,* 51–55.

Glines, D. (1989, December 20). Semi-autonomous teams in the San Diego Zoo. Unpublished report.

Stewart, T.A. (1992, May 18). The search for the organization of tomorrow. *Fortune,* 92–98.

CHAPTER 4

Cutcher-Gershenfield, J. (1988). *Tracing a transformation in industrial relations: The case of Xerox corporation and the Amalgated Clothing and Textile Workers Union.* Washington, D. C.: Department of Labor Bureau of Labor-Management Relations and Cooperative Programs.

Cutcher-Gershenfield, J. (1991). The impact of economic performance of a transformation in workplace relations. *Industrial and Labor Relations Review, 44,* 241–260.

CHAPTER 5

Bales, R.F. (1970). *Personality and interpersonal behavior.* New York: Holt, Rinehart, and Winston.

Fisher, B.A. (1974). *Small group decision-making.* New York: McGraw-Hill.

Goodall, H.L. (1990). *Small group communication in organizations.* Dubuque, IA: Wm. C. Brown.

Gorden, W.I., & Howe, R.J. (1977). *Team dynamics in developing organizations.* Dubuque, IA: Kendall/Hunt.

Gorden, W.I., & Nevins, R.J. (1993). *We mean business: Building communication competence in business and professions.* New York: Harper Collins.

Hirokawa, R.Y., & Pace, R. (1983). A descriptive investigation of the possible communication-based reasons for effective and ineffective group decision-making. *Communication Monographs, 50,* 363–379.

Kreps, G.L. (1986). *Organizational communication.* New York: Longman.

Tuckman, B.W. (1965). Developmental sequence in small groups. *Psychological Bulletin, 63,* 384–399.

CHAPTER 6

Dumaine, B. (1990, January 13). Creating a new company culture. *Fortune,* 127–132.

High Performance Work Practices and Firm Performance. (1993). U.S. Department of Labor.

Jacob, R. (1995, March 6). Corporate reputations. *Fortune,* 54–64.

Lewyn, M., Yang, D.J., Snadler, N., & Toy, S. (1992). Boeing: For want of a pin. *Business Week,* 96–97.

Loeb, M. (1995, March 20). Empowerment that pays off. *Fortune,* 145.

Stewart, T.A. (1995, March 20). Planning a career in a world without managers. *Fortune,* 72–80.

CHAPTERS 8 AND 9

Benne, K., & Sheats, P. (1948). Functional roles of group members. *Journal of Social Issues, 4,* 41–49.

Infante, D.I., Rancer, A.S., & Womack, D.F. (1993). *Building communication theory* (2d ed.). Prospect Heights, IL: Waveland Press.

Littlejohn, S. (1993). *Theories of human communication* (4th ed.). Belmont, CA: Wadsworth.

CHAPTER 10

Ferguson, S.D., & Ferguson, S. (1988). *Organizational communication* (2d ed.). New Brunswick, NJ: Transaction.

Prien, E. (1989). Measuring work setting characteristics: Basis for organizational development. *Human Resource Planning 12,* 331–337.

CHAPTER 11

Gibb, J. (1961). Defensive communication. *Journal of Communication, 11,* 141–148.

Goldhaber, G.M. (1990). *Organizational communication* (5th ed). Dubuque, IA: Wm. C. Brown.

CHAPTER 12

Hardin, G., & Baden, J. (1977). *Managing the commons.* New York: W. H. Freeman.

CHAPTER 13

Argyris, C. (1965). *Organization and innovation.* Homewood, IL: Richard D. Irwin.

Gorden, W.I., & Howe, R.J. (1977). *Team dynamics in developing organizations.* Dubuque, IA: Kendall/Hunt.

Likert, R. (1967). *The human organization.* New York: McGraw-Hill.

CHAPTER 15

Peale, N.V. (1967). *Enthusiasm makes the difference.* Carmel, NY: Guidepost Associates.

Peale, N.V. (1974). *The positive principle.* London: Prentice Hall International.

CHAPTER 17

DeVito, J.A. (1995). *Interpersonal communication* (7th ed.). New York: Harper Collins.

CHAPTERS 18 AND 19

Adler, R.B., & Towne, N. (1989). *Looking out, looking in* (6th ed). New York: Holt, Rinehart, and Winston.

Gorden, W.I., & Miller, J.R. (1983). *Managing your communication: In and for the organization.* Prospect Heights, IL: Waveland Press.

CHAPTER 20

Berger, C., & Calabrese, J.R. (1975). Some explorations in initial interaction and beyond: Toward a developmental theory of interpersonal communication. *Human Communication Research, 1,* 99–112.

CHAPTER 21

Barker, L., et al. (1991). *Groups in process: An introduction to small group communication.* Englewood Cliffs, NJ: Prentice Hall.

CHAPTER 22

Cragan, J.F., & Wright, D.W. (1991). *Communication in small group discussions.* St. Paul, MN: West.

CHAPTER 23

Pokras, S. (1987). *Systematic problem-solving and decision-making.* Los Altos, CA: Crisp Publications.

Training Resources Associates. (1984). *Session builders.* Harrisburg, PA: Training Resources Associates.

CHAPTER 24

Bemowski, K. (1994, October). Ford chairman was, and continues to be, a progress chaser. *Quality Progress,* 29–32.

CHAPTER 26

Janis, I.L. (1972). *Victims of groupthink: A psychological study of foreign-policy decisions and fiascoes.* Boston: Houghton Mifflin.

CHAPTER 27

Baum, H. (1989). Organizational politics against organizational culture: A psychoanalytic perspective. *Human Resource Management, 28,* 191–206.

Block, B. (1989). Creating a culture all employees can accept. *Management Review, 78,* 41–45.

Burack, E. (1991). Changing the company culture—the role of human resource development. *Long Range Planning, 24,* 88–95.

Sackmann, S. (1989). The role of metaphors in the organization transformation. *Human Relations, 42,* 463–485.

CHAPTER 28

Kiechel, W. (1993, May 17). How we will work in the year 2000. *Fortune,* 38–52.

CHAPTER 29

Leathers, D. (1986). *Successful nonverbal communication: Principles and applications.* New York: Macmillan.

CHAPTERS 30–34

Arensberg, C. (1951). Behavior and organization: Industrial studies. In J. H. Roher & M. Sherif (Eds.)., *Social psychology at the crossroads* (pp. 324–352). New York: Harper and Row.

Argyris, C. (1965). *Organization and innovation.* Homewood, IL: Richard D. Irwin.

Argyris, C. (1966). Interpersonal barriers to decision making. *Harvard Business Review, 44,* 84–97.

Argyris, C. (1971). *Management and organizational development.* New York: McGraw-Hill.

Auer, P., & Riegler, C. (1990). *Post-Taylorism: The enterprise as a place of learning organizational change—A comprehensive study on work changes and its context at VOLVO* (S. Schenck & K. Shire, Trans.). Sweden: Libergraf AB.

Bell, D. (1988). *Bringing your employees into the business: An employee ownership handbook for small business.* Kent, OH: Kent Popular Press.

Blake, R.R., & Mouton, J.S. (1964). *The managerial grid.* Houston, TX: Gulf.

Blake, R.R., & Mouton, J.S. (1968). *Corporate excellence through grid organizational development.* Houston, TX: Gulf.

Bucklow, M. (1966). A new role for the work group. *Administrative Science Quarterly, 11,* 59–78.

Buller, P.F., & Bell, C.H. (1986). Effects of team building and goal setting on productivity: A field experiment. *Academy of Management Journal, 29,* 305–328.

Coch, L., & French, J.R.P. (1948). Overcoming resistance to change. *Human Relations, 1,* 512–532.

Collins, O., Dalton, M., & Roy, D. (1946). Restriction of output and social cleavage in industry. *Applied Anthropology, 5,* 1–14.

Dalton, M. (1959). *Men who manage.* New York: Wiley.

Drago, R. (1988). Quality circle survival: An exploratory analysis. *Industrial Relations, 27,* 336–351.

Dunphy, D. (1972). *The primary group: A handbook for analysis and field research.* New York: Appleton-Century-Crofts.

Ferris, G. R., & Wagner, J. A. (1985). Quality circles in the United States: A conceptual reevaluation. *Journal of Applied Behavioral Science, 21,* 155–167.

French, J., Kornhauser, A., & Marrow, A. (1946). Conflict and cooperation in industry. *Journal of Social Issues, 2,* 29–34.

French, J., Israel, J., & Äs, D. (1960). An experiment in participation in a Norwegian factory: Interpersonal dimension of decision-making. *Human Relations, 13,* 3–19.

Gorden, W.I. (1979). Experiential training: A comparison of T-group, Tavistock, and EST. *Communication Education, 28,* 39–48.

Gorden, W.I. (1994). 'Wego' comes in several varieties and is not simple. *Communication Yearbook, 17,* 285–297.

Gorden, W.I., Holmberg, K., & Heisey, D.R. (1994). Equity and the Swedish work environment. *Employee Responsibilities and Rights Journal, 7,* 1–20.

Harrison, T.M. (1994). Communication and interdependence in democratic organizations. *Communication Yearbook, 17*, 247–274.

Homans, G.C. (1950). *The human group.* New York: Harcourt, Brace, and World.

Homans, G.C. (1954). The cash posters: A study of a group of work girls. *American Sociological Review, 19,* 724–733.

Horsfall, A., & Arensberg, C. (1949). Teamwork and productivity in a shoe factory. *Human Organization, 8,* 13–25.

Kornbluh, H. (1984). Work place democracy and quality of work life: Problems and prospects. *Annals of the American Academy of Political and Social Science, 473,* 88–95.

Lawler, E.E., Mohrman, S., & Ledford, G.E. (1992). The Fortune 1000 and total quality. *Journal for Quality and Participation, 15,* 6–10.

Logue, J., Quilligan, J.B., & Weissmann, B.J. (1985). *BUYOUT! Employee ownership as an alternative to plant shutdowns: The Ohio experience.* Kent, OH: Kent Popular Press.

Lupton, T. (1966). *Management and the social sciences.* London: Hutchinson & Company.

Maier, N.R.F. (1953). An experimental test of the effect of training on discussion leadership. *Human Relations, 6,* 161–173.

Marrow, A. (1948). Group dynamics in industry: Implications for guidance and personnel workers. *Occupations, 26,* 472–476.

Marrow, A.J., Bowers, D.G., & Seashore, S.E. (1967). *Management by participation: Creating a climate for personal and organizational development.* New York: Harper and Row.

Mayo, E. (1924–25) Revery and industrial fatigue. *Journal of Personnel Research, 3,* 273–287.

Mayo, E. (1946). *The human problems of an industrial civilization* (2d ed.). New York: Macmillan.

Mayo, E., & Lombard, G. (1944). *Teamwork and labor turnover in the aircraft industry of Southern California.* Boston: Graduate School of Business Administration.

Mohr, W.L., & Mohr, H. (1983). *Quality circles changing images of people at work.* Boston: Addison-Wesley.

Roethlisberger, F. J. (1941). *Management and morale.* Cambridge, MA: Harvard University Press.

Roethlisberger, F.J., & Dickson, W. (1939). *Management and the workers: Social versus technical organization in industry.* Cambridge, MA: Harvard University Press.

Roy, D. (1952). Quota restrictions and goldbricking in a machine shop. *American Journal of Sociology, 57,* 427–432.

Rubinstein, S., Bennett, M, & Kochan, T. (1993). The Saturn partnership: Co-Management and the reinvention of the local union. In B.E. Kaufman & M. M. Kleiner (Eds.), *Employee representation: Alternatives and future directions* (pp. 339–370). Madison, WI: Industrial Relations Research Association.

Schacter, H.L. (1989). Frederick Winslow Taylor and the idea of workers participation. *Administration & Society, 21,* 20–30.

Seashore, S.E. (1954). *Group cohesiveness in the industrial work group.* Ann Arbor, MI: Survey Research Center Institute for Social Research.

Seashore, S.E. (1964). Field experiments with formal organizations. *Human Organization, 23,* 164–170.

Smith, P.B. (1973). *Groups within organizations: Applications of social psychology to organizational behavior.* New York: Harper and Row.

Söderlund, S. (1987). *Working environment in Sweden: A question of partnership.* Swedish Work Environment Fund.

Sofer, C. (1972). *Organizations in theory and practice.* New York: Basic Books.

Steel, R.P., & Lloyd, R.F. (1988). Cognitive, affective, and behavioral outcomes of participation in quality circles: Conceptual and empirical findings. *Journal of Applied Behavioral Science, 24,* 1–17.

Stohl, C., & Jennings, K. (1988). Volunteerism and voice in quality circles. *Western Journal of Speech Communication, 52,* 238–251.

Sundstrom, E., DeMeuse, K.P., & Futrell, D. (1990). Work teams: Applications and effectiveness. *American Psychologist, 45,* 120–133.

Taylor, F.W. (1911). *Principles of scientific management.* New York: Harper and Brothers.

Trist, E., & Bamforth, K. (1951). Some social and psychological consequences of the longwall method of coal getting. *Human Relations, 4,* 3–30.

Trist, E., Higgin, G., Murray, H., & Pollack, A. (1963). *Organizational choice: Capabilities of groups at the coal face under changing technologies.* London: Tavistock.

Walker, C., & Guest, R. (1952). *The man on the assembly line.* Cambridge, MA: Harvard University Press.

Weick, K. (1966). The concept of equity in the perception of pay. *Administrative Science Quarterly, 21,* 1–19.

Whitsett, D.A., & Yorks, L. (1983). *From management theory to business sense.* New York: AMACOM.

Whyte, W.F. (1951). Small groups in large organizations. In J. H. Roher & M. Sherif (Eds)., *Social psychology at the crossroads* (pp. 297–312). New York: Harper Brothers.

Wolfe, D.R., Hauck, W.C., & Varney, G.H. (1984). Quality circles: The U.S. experience. *Proceedings of the 27th Annual Conference Midwest Academy of Management.* Mimeographed copy.

Wood, R., Hull, F., & Azumi, K. (1983). Evaluating quality circles: The American application. *California Management Review, 26,* 37–51.

Index

A

ABC Shoe Factory, study of, 139-140
Advice, how to give, 81
Agendas, communcation, 22
Aircraft industry, studies of, 145
Amalgamated Clothing and Textile Workers Union (ACTWU), 19
Analysis, 163
  force field, 110, 146
  how to use, 81
Applied Anthropology (Collins, Dalton, Roy), 143
Arensberg, Conrad, 135-137, 139, 149
Argyris, Chris, 12, 61, 157, 161
  Organization and Innovation, 158
Äs, D., 154
Assembly-line workers, study of, 149-150, 165-166
Associates at work, 91-92
Attributes of a system, 41
Auer, P., 165-166

B

Bakke, E. W., 135
Bakke, W. Wight, 149
Barbato, Carole A., v, vi
Bavelas, Alex, 145-146
Bell, C. H., 164
Benchmark, 20
Benchmarking, process of, 20
Biases, guarding against, 85
Bion, W. R., 155
Blake, R. R., 157
  The Managerial Grid, 11
Block, Barbara, 121
Boeing, management history of, 28-29
Bowers, D. G., 153
Brainstorming, 110, 163
Bucklow, M., 155-157
Buller, P. F., 164
Business organizations. *See also* Management practices
  communication in. *See* Communication
  culture of
    changing, 121-122
    decision-making, 163
    readiness, 28-29
  decision-making in. *See* Decision-making
  employee morale of. *See also* Employees
    creating enthusiasm, 65, 67-68
    economic incentives, 139-140, 143

Business organizations—*Cont.*
  need for control, 136-138, 147
  and setting goals, 65. *See also* Work groups, conflicting goals of
  theories of, 151-152
  go team *vs.* not go team, 29-30
  interaction with environment, 42
  managing work settings of, 49
  personalities in, dealing with, 95. *See also* Ego, interference from
  process of development of, 121-122
  restructuring of, 28
  spirit of, 61-62
  steering committee of, 31
  system of
    elements, 41-42
    principles of operation, 45-46
  workspace in, delegation of, 127-128

C

Case studies, 163
Cash posters, study of, 150-151
Cause-effect diagrams, 163
Change, workers' resistance to, 146-147
The Change Masters (Kanter), 12
Chapple, Eliot, 135, 139
Checksheets, 163
Cheerleader role, 99
Chrysler, teamwork at, 27
Civility, use of, 99
Cliches, formation of, 150-151
Coal mining workers, studies of, 156, 158
Coch, Lester, 146-147
Codetermination, 164
Cohen (reference), 167
Cohesiveness, 151-152
Collaborative quality effort, 31
Collins, Orvis, 144-145
  Applied Anthropology, 143
Communication
  and behavioral roles, 99
  climates of, 51-52
  and consensus decisions, 113
  cycles of, 9-10, 22-24
  employee-communications circles, 161-162
  and employee volunteerism, 163-164
  feedback devises in, 81-82
  and listening, 77-78, 81, 85-86

Communication—*Cont.*
  between management and teams, 49
  nonverbal, 127, 131
  and presentations, 71
  self-interest, 25
  and team relationships, 23-25, 91-92, 95
  within teams, 12-13, 16-17, 22, 131
  and teamthink, 4, 115-116
Competition in business, 61
Conflict phase, 25-26
Consensus, operating by, 23, 109-110, 113
Control, employee need for, 136-138, 147
Coon (reference), 139
Cooperatives, employee owned, 167
Corporate culture. *See also* Business organizations
  changing, 121-122
  and decision-making, 163
  readiness of, 28-29
Corporations, employee owned, 167
Creativity within teams, 12
Critical evaluator, 115
Cutcher-Gershenfield, Joel, 19

D

Dalton, Melville, 144
  Applied Anthropology, 143
Data collection, 163
Decision-making
  by consensus, 113
  criteria of, 105
  and organizational culture, 163
  participation in, 147, 168-169
  at Saturn Corp., 166
  within teams, 7-9
  tools for, 109-110
DeMeuse, K. P., 161
Deming, W. Edward, 161
Democracy
  in employee-owned businesses, 167
  within teams, 9
  vs. consensus, 113
  workplace, 163
    in Scandinavia, 164
Derry, Robbin, 9
Devil's advocate role, 99
Diagrams
  cause-effect, 163
  fishbone, 13, 110
  Pareto, 163
  scatter, 163
Dickson, W., 137
"Direct relevancy" of participation, 154
"Doctrine of information organization or teamwork", 137
Donovan, James, 162
Drago, R., 164
Durkheim (reference), 136
Dygert, Charles, 9

Dynamics of teams, 8-10
  communication cycles, 22-23
  inclusion, 21
  phases, 25-26
  power, 21-22
  relationship track, 23-24, 95
  roles, 24-25, 95, 99
  task track, 23, 95
  values, 22

E

Eaton, Bob, 27
Economic incentives, 139-140, 143
Ego, interference from, 81-82
Emergence phase, 25
Employees. *See also* Teams; Work groups
  communication circles of, 161-162
  expectations of, 164
  involvement groups of, 11, 161, 163
  and layoffs, 19
  morale of
    creating enthusiasm, 65, 67-68
    economic incentives, 139-140, 143
    and setting goals, 65. *See also* Work groups, conflicting goals of
  theories of, 151-152
  need for control, 136-138, 147
  ownership programs, 167
  participation of, 161-163
  volunteerism, 163-164
Employee stock ownership plans (ESOP), 167
"Empowering" the individual, 121
Enthusiasm, developing, 65, 67-68
Environment, system interaction with, 42
Equifinality, principle of, 46
Esso Company, study by, 157
Exchange theory, 151

F

Facial expressions, interpreting, 131
Feasibility studies, 29-30
Feedback
  devices for, 81-82
  importance of, 138
Ferris, G. R., 163
Finagle's law, 109
Fishbone diagram, 13, 110
Flight behavior in work groups, 155-156
Force field theory, 110, 146
Ford company
  management history of, 28
  teamwork at, 110
"Formal organization" of work groups, 136
Fortune, 28, 127-128, 162-163
French, John R. P., 145-147, 154

Friendly world values, 22
Friendships at work, 91-92. *See also* Relationships, workplace
Futrell, D., 161
"Gamesmanship" of work groups, 157

G

General Electric, teamwork at, 6-8
General Motors, teamwork at, 8
Glines, David, 15-17
Gorden, William I., v, 164
Graphs, use of, 163
Great Britain, work groups research in, 155-156
Greenlight brainstorming, 110
Group Cohesiveness in the Industrial Work Group (Seashore), 151
Group interpersonal competence. *See* teamness, signs of
Groups. *See* Work groups
Groupthink, dangers of, 115-116
Guest, Robert H., 149

H

Harden, Garret, 55
Harrison, T. M., 167
Harvard Business Review, 157
Harvard University, research by, 135-138
Harwood Company, studies of, 145-147, 153, 158
Hawthorne experiments, 137-139
Herzberg (reference), 161
Hidden agendas, 22
High Performance Work Practices and Firm Performance (U.S. Dept. of Labor), 20
Histograms, 163
Homans, George, 135, 138-139, 151
   The Human Group, 150
Horsfall, Alexander, 139-140
How to Become Happily Employed (Block), 121
"Human component" in organizations, 136
The Human Group (Homans), 150
Humanization of workplace, 165
Human nature, 8-9
The Human Side of Enterprise (McGregor), 11
"Illumination studies", 137

I

Individualism, 22
"Informal organization" of work groups, 140
Information provider role, 99
In-groups, 21, 140, 169
Interactionist philosophy, 139-140
Interdependence, principle of, 45
International Association of Quality Circles (IAQC), 162
Ishikawa, Kaoru, 161
Isolation, impact of, on workers, 149, 151
Israel, J., 154

J

Japan
   quality circles of, 161-162
   teamwork in, 61
Japanese Union of Scientists and Engineers (JUSE), 161
Jaques, Elliot, 155-156
Jennings, K., 163-164
Journal of Personnel Research, 136
Judgements
   how to make, 81
   reserving, 85
Juran, Joseph M., 161-162
Jusela, Gary, 28-29

K

Kanter, Rosabeth Moss, 12
Katz, Daniel, 135
Katzenbach, Jon, 6
Kearns, David, 20
Key input/output variables, 13

L

Labor, division of, 135-136
Labor-management relations. *See also* Management practices
   at Saturn Corp., 166
   Swedish model of, 164
   at Xerox, 19
Lawler, E. E., 162-163
Leadership in teams, 11, 85, 99
Lewin, Kurt, 135, 145-146, 155, 157
Likert, Rensis, 153, 155, 157, 161
   New Patterns of Management, 12
Linking-pin theory, 155
Listening skills, 77-78, 81, 85-86
Lloyd, R. F., 162
Lockheed, quality circles at, 162
Logue, J., 167
Lombard, G., 145
Lupton, T., 149, 156

M

MacArthur, Douglas, 161
McGregor, Douglas, 155, 161
   The Human Side of Enterprise, 11
McKinsey and Company, 9
Maier, N. R. F., 155
Malcolm Baldrige National Quality Award, 20
Malinowski (reference), 136
Management by Participation: Creating a Climate for Personal and Organizational Development (Marrow, Bowers & Seashore), 153
Management practices. *See also* Business organizations
   behavior, 157-158
   benchmarking, 20

Management practices—*Cont.*
 communication. *See* Communication
 and employee layoffs, 19
 facts *vs.* opinions, 20
 participation, 153-155
 styles, 153
 total quality management, 31, 163
 traditional *vs.* transformational, 19-20
Managerial grid, 157
The Managerial Grid (Blake and Mouton), 11
Man on the Assembly Line (Walker & Guest), 149
Marrow, Alfred, 145-146
 *Management by Participation: Creating a Climate for
  –Personal and Organizational Development*, 153
Mayo, Elton, 11, 135-139, 145, 157
Menzies, I. E. P., 155-156
Mohr, H., 163
Mohr, W. L., 163
Morale, employee
 creating enthusiasm, 65, 67-68
 economic incentives, 139-140, 143
 need for control, 136-138, 147
 and setting goals, 65
 theories of, 151-152
Moreno, J. L., 135
Motivation, developing, 65, 67-68
Motorola, teamwork at, 28
Mouton, J. S., 11, 157
 The Managerial Grid, 11
Murphy's law, 109
Myers, Doug, 16
Myers, Scott A., v

N

Nagle, Erica L., v
National Research Council, study of, 137
National Training Laboritories (NTL), 155, 157-158
New Patterns of Management (Likert), 12
New United Motor Manufacturing Inc. (NUMMI),
 teamwork at, 27-28
Nonsummativity, principle of, 45
North, south, east, west model, 30
Norwegian Shoe Factory, study of, 154

O

Objects of a system, 41
Open-mindedness, 85
Organizational chart, 42
Organizational Choice (Trist), 156
Organizational transformation, 121-122
Organization and Innovation (Argyris), 158
Organizations. *See* Business organizations
Orientation phase, 25
Outcome scenarios, 110
Out-groups, 21
Oversight teams, 14

P

Paraphrasing, purpose of, 82
Pareto diagrams, 163
Participation
 in decision-making, 147, 168-169
 "direct relevancy" of, 154
 employee, 161-163
 management, 153-155
People, catetories of, 91
Personalities, dealing with, 95. *See also* Ego,
 interference from
Phase development, 25-26
Philadelphia Textile Mill, research of, 136-137
Plan, test, act sequence, 110
Plan-do-check-act model, 14
Power within teams, 21-22
Prejudice, guarding against, 85
Presentations, spoken, 71
Principles of Scientific Management (Taylor), 135
Problem-solving. *See also* quality circles
 analytical, 13-14
 and decision-making, 105
 and group development, 26
 and groupthink, 115-116
 tools for, 109-110
Productivity
 improvement of, 167
 influences on, 153-155
 in U.S., 162
Prompting, when to use, 82
Proxemics, concept of, 128
Puckett, John, 7
Putnam, M. L., 138

Q

Quality, quest for, 13-14
Quality circles, 15, 161-164
Quality-of-work-life (QWL)
 committees, 163
 program at Saturn Corp., 166
 research, 164
Quarrey (reference), 167
Question, how to, 81

R

Radcliffe-Brown (reference), 136
Reach-test spiral, 24
Reese, Rich J., 16
Reinforcement phase, 25
Relationships
 system, 41-42
 workplace, 23-25, 91-92, 95
The Renewal Factor (Waterman), 12
Responsibility committees, 14
Riegler, C., 165-166
Roethlisberger, F. J., 137

Roles, group. *See* Work groups, roles of
Roy, Donald, 143
Rubbermaid, teamwork at, 28

S

Saltsjöbaden Agreement, 164
Samaeul in Korea, 162
Sampling, 163
San Diego Zoo, teamwork at, 15-17
Saturn, quality-of-work-life at, 166
Scandinavia, socio-technical experiments of, 164-166
Scatter diagrams, 163
Scenarios, outcome, 110
Schmitt, Wolfgang, 28
Seashore, Stanley, 135, 139, 152
   Group Cohesiveness in the Industrial Work Group, 151
   Management by Participation: Creating a Climate for Personal and Organizational Development, 153
Security of Employment Act, 164
Self-interest roles, 95
Self-regulation, principle of, 45-46
Shepard, H. A., 157
Signs of teamness, 12, 61, 158
Skull sessions, 13
Smith, Douglas, 6
Smith, P. B., 154
"Social geography" of work groups, 149
Socio-psychological system of work groups, 156
Sofer, C., 138, 155-156
Space, importance of, 127-128
Speaking skills, learning, 71
Statistical quality control (SQC), 161
Steel, R. P., 162
Stohl, C., 163-164
Success Is A Team Effort (Dygert), 9
Sundstrom, E., 161
Supervision, workplace, 136
Supportive, how to be, 81-82
Surveys, organizationwide, 16-17
Swedish Leadership Organization and Codetermination Program (LOM), 164-165
System, elements of, 41-42
"Systematic soldiering" of work groups, 136
System 4 Participative Management, 12, 153

T

Task
   accomplishment, 23-24
   leader role, 99
   track, 23
Tavistock Institute, studies by, 155-158, 164-165
Taylor, Frederick W., 136, 139, 165
   Principles of Scientific Management, 135
Teamness, signs of, 12, 61, 158
Teams. *See also* Employees; Teamwork; Work groups
   abuse of, 3-4, 7
   accountability within, 10, 31

Teams—*Cont.*
   awareness campaigns of, 31
   benefits of being on, 71
   building of, 8, 32, 61
   characteristic behavior of, 6-7
   communication within. *See* Communication
   concepts of, 3-4, 12, 61, 99
   configurations of, 27
   consensus, operating by, 23, 109-110, 113
   creativity within, 12
   and cross-training, 9, 25
   and decision-making. *See* Decision-making
   democracy in, 9. *See also* Democracy
   and doing right, 14
   dynamics of. *See* Dynamics of teams
   feasibility of, 29-30
   goals of, 5-6, 65. *See also* Work groups, conflicting goals of
   and greed *vs.* fairness, 9
   and human nature, 8-9
   and human resources, 27
   and individual *vs.* group worth, 11-12
   ingredients of, 45
   kinds of, 6
   leadership of, 11, 85, 99
   oversight, 14
   performance rewards for, 9
   personalities within, 95. *See also* Ego, interference from
   principles of operation of, 45-46
   and problem-solving. *See* Problem-solving
   process needs of, 10
   project work, 28
   purposes of, 4-5
   reasons for failure of, 109
   relationships within, 23-25, 91-92, 95
   self-assessments of, 12, 99
   self-directed, 16, 32, 109
   sizes of, 5
   skull sessions of, 13
   spirit of, 61
   in sports, 3, 11, 21, 27
   and stress *vs.* fear, 9
   structural, 27
   and supportive atmosphere, 12
   technological, 27
   training of, 32
   values of, 22
   vs. chain of command, 6-7, 31
   vs. work groups, 5, 22, 24, 61
   and workspace, 127-128
Teamsters Union, 15
Teamthink, dangers of, 4, 115-116
Teamwork, 4-5
   evolution of, 162-163
   spirit of, 61
Teamwork training
   circle of meaning, 36f
   objectives of, 110
   seminar participants, 36f

Teamwork training—*Cont.*
  trainer, responsibilities of, vii, 35-36
  workout exercises
    active listening, 87
    brainstorming, 63
    communication awareness, 50
    communication climate, 53
    critical listening, 79-80
    decision-making, 106-107, 114
    enthusiasm, 69
    feedback processes, 83
    group interest, 56-57
    materials needed for, 37f
    nonverbal messages, 132
    organizational transformation, 123-124
    personality and work roles, 96-97
    presentations, principles of, 72-73
    problem-solving, 111
    proxemics, 129
    role playing, 100-101
    setting goals, 66
    system operation principles, 47
    team interdependence, 56
    teamthink, 117
    understanding system, 43
    working relationships, 93
Team Xerox, 19
"Temporary society", 61
Tension releaser role, 99
T-groups, 157-159
Theories
  exchange, 151
  force field, 146
  linking-pin, 155
  small-group process, 155
  Theory X, 136
Tokyo University, studies by, 161
Total quality control, 161
Total quality management, 31, 163
"Tragedy of the commons", 55
Trainers, use of, 145-146
Training, teamwork. *See* Teamwork training
Training groups (T-groups), 157-159
Transactional role playing, 99
Transformation, organizational, 121-122
Transformational practices, 19-20
Trist, Eric, 156
Trotman, Alex, 110
Trust, importance of, 91-92

U

Unions, workers. *See* Workers unions
United States Department of Labor
  on American work practices, 27
  High Performance Work Practices and Firm Performance, 20
University of Chicago, studies by, 143-145
University of Texas, study by, 157

V

Vans, teamwork at, 7-8
Variables, key input/output, 13
Visible agendas, 22
Volunteerism, employee, 163-164
Volvo, work group experiments at, 165-166

W

Wagner, J. A., 163
Walker, Charles, 135
  Man on the Assembly Line, 149
Waterman, Robert, 12
Western Electric Company, experiments at, 137-138
Whyte, William, 135, 139
The Wisdom of Teams (Katzenbach and Smith), 6
Wood, R., 162
Work councils of Sweden, 161-162
Work Environment Act, 164
Workers unions
  Amalgamated Clothing and Textile Workers Union (ACTWU), 19
  Teamsters Union, 15
Work ethic, individual, 22
Work groups. *See also* Employees; Teams
  autonomous, 156-157, 164-166
  cohesiveness of, 151-152
  conflicting goals of, 138-140, 143-146
  description of, 150
  flight behavior in, 155-156
  "formal organization" of, 136
  formation of, 167-168
  "gamesmanship" of, 157
  and human behavior, 158-159
  influence of, in industry, 147
  "informal organization" of, 140
  norms, creation of, 140-141
  and productivity, 155
  research on
    ABC Shoe Factory, 139-140
    aircraft industry studies, 145
    assembly-line study, 149-150, 165-166
    cash posters study, 150-151
    Chicago factory studies, 143-145
    conclusions drawn from, 167-169
    earliest, 135-136
    employee ownership programs, 167
    Harwood Company studies, 145-147, 153, 158
    Hawthorne experiments, 137-139
    Midwest Machine Company, 151-152
    Norwegian Shoe Factory, 154
    NTL studies on T-groups, 157-159
    Philadelphia Textile Mill, 136-137
    quality circles, 161-164
    at Saturn Corp., 166
    socio-technical concepts, 164-166
    Tavistock Institute, 155-158
    Theory X, 136

Work groups.—*Cont.*
　　Weldon Company, 153-154
　resistance to change, 146-147
　roles of, 24-25, 95, 99
　social element of, 149-151
　"social geography" of, 149
　socio-psychological system of, 156
　"systematic soldiering" of, 136
　and technology, 149-150, 152, 165-166
　vs. teams, 5, 22, 24, 61
Workout session, business application of, vii. *See also*
　　Teamwork training, workout exercises
Workplace, humanization of, 165

Work-settings, elements of managing, 49
Workspace, importance of, 127-128

X

XEL Communications Inc., teamwork at, 7
Xerox, management history of, 19-20

Y

Yale University, study by, 149-150

Thank you for choosing Irwin Professional Publishing for your information needs. If you are part of a corporation, professional association, or government agency, consider our newest option: Irwin Professional Custom Publishing. This service helps you create customized books, manuals, and other materials from your organization's resources, select chapters of our books, or both.

Irwin Professional Publishing books are also excellent resources for training/educational programs, premiums, and incentives. For information on volume discounts or Custom Publishing, call 1-800-634-3966.

Other books of interest to you from Irwin Professional Publishing...

DIVERSE TEAMS AT WORK

Capitalizing on the Power of Diversity

Lee Gardenswartz and Anita Rowe

Provides guidelines for building and managing teams with members from a variety of backgrounds, including tips on how to resolve conflicts, solve problems, and make decisions as a highly diverse group.
0-7863-0425-1   175 pages

WHY TEAMS FAIL

And What To Do About It

Darcy E. Hitchcock and Marsha L. Willard

Identifies the most common problems faced by teams, offering specific suggestions for spotting and solving the problems and creating teams that really work.
0-7863-0423-5   225 pages

LEADING TEAMS

Mastering the New Role

John H. Zenger, Ed Musselwhite, Kathleen Hurson, and Craig Perrin

Focuses specifically on the role of the leader as the key to long-term success, showing how managers can carve an enduring, vital position for themselves in a team environment.
1-55623-894-0   275 pages